THE MAKING OF A MAN

THE MAKING OF A MAN

Notes on Transsexuality

MAXIM FEBRUARI

Translation by Andy Brown

REAKTION BOOKS

Published by Reaktion Books Ltd
33 Great Sutton Street
London EC1V 0DX, UK
www.reaktionbooks.co.uk

First published in Dutch as
De Maakbare Man: Notities over Transseksualiteit
by Prometheus, Amsterdam, 2013
© Maxim Februari 2013

English-language translation by Andy Brown
Translation copyright © Reaktion Books 2015

The publisher gratefully acknowledges the support of the
Dutch Foundation for Literature

Printed and bound in Great Britain
by TJ International, Padstow, Cornwall

A catalogue record for this book is available from the British Library

ISBN 978 1 78023 444 1

Contents

Preface

When I announced in the autumn of 2012 that from then on I was going to live as a man, no one batted an eyelid. Official bodies seemed singularly unimpressed; distant relatives responded as if it were the most natural thing in the world. Work kept coming in and my private life just carried on. Apart from considerate officials calling me 'sir' rather than 'madam', nothing changed at all.

When I announced in the autumn of 2012 that from then on I was going to live as a man, all hell broke loose. Television and radio presenters wanted to talk to me about operations, journalists called with questions about my sex life and complete strangers showed interest in the intimate parts of my body because they wanted to write papers on it. I was frequently baffled.

When I announced in the autumn of 2012 that from then on I was going to live as a man, everyone suddenly became very wary. Before conversations

I was assured that of course I did not have to say anything I didn't want to, and I saw people searching desperately for the right words. How was it going with my transi- . . . transse- . . . trans-what? It was as if I had joined a radical sect which forbade me to talk to outsiders. Occasionally someone would express these concerns out loud, asking: 'I assume you have kept your sense of humour?'

If you want to know what really happened, you need to realize that all three versions of the story are true. On the whole, everyday life just went on, but now and again my transition from woman to man came up – and then conversations became both more polite and more impolite. Some people became more uncomfortable, while others simply became ruder.

I soon realized that this wasn't constructive. Transsexuality is just beginning to attract attention from society at large and if I can contribute to a better understanding of what it means, I am willing to say something about my body and my feelings (which interviewers like to say I have been 'grappling with'). But I prefer to talk about the meaning of sex in society, about legal regulations and social relations. That is why I decided to write down the answers to the most frequently asked – and unasked – questions.

What I have written here is all that I know. That is quite a lot, but not everything. It is explicitly not my intention to tell a definitive story that can be used as some kind of catechism. I have collected these notes in the hope that they can help in personal or social conversations, so that talking about transsexuality will not remain stuck in shame and shamelessness.

one

Identity: Gender and Sex

NOT LONG AGO, I visited the Dutch Poultry Museum in Barneveld, where I spent a while looking at some certificates in a display case. In the 1940s, with the help of Japanese experts, prominent Barneveld citizens set up a school where students were taught how to determine the sex of a chick. In the display case was a list of sexers who had successfully completed their training at the Sexing School in Barneveld in the academic years of 1947 and 1948. The examination requirements were very clearly specified:

CERTIFICATE A:
Sexing 200 chicks in a maximum of 20 minutes with a 95 per cent certainty for both sexes

CERTIFICATE B:
Sexing 200 chicks in a maximum of 30 minutes with a 95 per cent certainty for both sexes

Sexing 200 chicks in a maximum of 40 minutes
with 90 per cent certainty for hens and 95 per cent
certainty for cocks

We live under the illusion that we can classify everyone
as male or female, and that we can do so almost beyond
the shadow of a doubt. But here was the evidence of
a serious course of study in which students received
extensive lessons in distinguishing the sexes of chickens,
and yet there still proved to be a wide margin of
uncertainty. Imagine that the chicks themselves had
had a say in the matter about what gender they felt they
belonged to, and about their deep inner convictions
regarding their masculinity or femininity. That would
have completely shattered the illusion of certainty.

Sex and gender

In 1907, in his epilogue to the autobiography of the
transsexual author Karl Baer, the doctor Magnus
Hirschfeld wrote that 'a person's gender has more to
do with their soul than with their body. Or, in more
medical terms, with their brain than with their genitals.'

With these words Hirschfeld touched on the
difference between sex and gender, even before the terms
for this distinction had become current. Sex is what sexers
try to determine by studying your genitals, your body
and your chromosomes; gender is the mental, immaterial

aspect of your sexuality, how you see yourself and how others see you. For Hirschfeld, who was a pioneer in the field of transsexuality, what particularly mattered was his patients' *Geschlechtszugehörigkeitsgefühl*, the gender they felt they belonged to. With medical treatment you can try to make your body match that gender.

You are who you are

Outsiders who are interested in your gender identity can of course ask how you yourself experience it. But if they want to know the ins and outs without your help, they have to go by your behaviour and the signals you send out. On a psychologist's form, I was once asked if I played boys' or girls' games when I was a child. Everyone I told about this was able to guess my answer: 'I read.'

Of course, I could dig up endless anecdotes from my childhood if experts were to ask me to prove that I really am a man and that I always have been. But your identity is not something you have to prove. Identity actually just means that you are who you are, and that is no one else's business. To put psychologists' minds at rest, I am happy to tell them about the moments when it suddenly became clear to me who I was. Like the afternoon when a girlfriend suggested that we play mummies and daddies, for want of anything better, and asked me who I wanted to be. Sitting on the blue lino in our house, I replied in a blaze of indignation: 'I'm always the daddy. I'm never the mummy.' But in fact these are recollections of my *Geschlechtszugehörigkeitsgefühl*, not proof that I was right and that it was true that I was always the daddy and never the mummy.

Gender dysphoria, the feeling that something is wrong with the role you have been allotted (dysphoria is the opposite from euphoria), cannot be measured, demonstrated or proved. I can still recall how bewildered I was when, at the age of four or five, I unwrapped a present from my grandmother and found myself holding a dustpan and brush. But what does this story really demonstrate? My aversion to the dustpan and brush could just as well have been an indication of a sensible feminist disposition.

That is why I think the question concerning my 'boyishness' is off-target. There are many women who describe themselves as 'boyish', or 'tomboys'. In the course of my life I have met a lot of heterosexual and lesbian women who, as adults too, are much stronger and tougher than I am, but who are nevertheless perfectly happy to be women. I do not want sex reassignment therapy because I am manly, but because I am a man. How do I know that? Because of my *Geschlechtszugehörigkeitsgefühl*: the firm conviction that others are wrong when they think that I am a woman.

Let me tell one more story from my childhood, especially because it shows how extremely satisfied and happy you can become if you take a step in the right direction. It was the early 1970s and I must have been eight or nine years old. We were camping at a spot on the French Riviera where the visitors were still mainly French. Back in those days there was not much organized entertainment, so a beauty contest for the girls at the campsite was a big event.

During the day a stage was erected on an open field, causing much excitement among the campers. Night fell. It was dark and, if I remember correctly, banners advertising Ricard – THE REAL PASTIS FROM MARSEILLE – were hanging from the trees. The music had started and the girls were waiting in line to go on stage.

I wandered over. My fashion-conscious mother had made a rare exception and allowed me to wear a pair of trousers and a jumper belonging to my older brother.

The beauty queens filed onto the stage. They were wearing elaborate French dresses with frills. Curling tongs, powder boxes and eyebrow pencils had clearly been working overtime. And suddenly I saw myself standing there, in the middle of the audience, in those corduroy trousers, and I knew for certain that the next moment the whole crowd would turn around in unison to look at me and burst out in admiration at the way I was dressed: 'Wow, you look fantastic!' Because I did look fantastic. At least, I thought so myself. I even believe that I have never again looked as wonderful as I did that night in that jumper and those trousers.

Intersexuality

Throughout the years, it has been my firm conviction that you do not have to conform to the stereotype of masculinity to be a man, or to the stereotype of femininity to be a woman. That is why I have always been fascinated by the god Hermaphroditus, from whom the term 'hermaphrodite' originated. The first novel I wrote largely revolved around this two-sexed deity. The story goes that the god was chased by an amorous water nymph who was so madly in love with him that she asked the gods to merge their bodies. The gods granted her wish and that is how Hermaphroditus came to have an androgynous body.

Hermaphroditism was a popular theme in classical antiquity. Many sculptures portrayed deities with both male and female sexual characteristics. The first sculpture of this kind that I encountered had originally been part of the art collection in the Villa Borghese in Rome, but had been bought by Napoleon and ended up in Paris, and ultimately the Louvre. According to Horace Walpole, at the beginning of the eighteenth century his aunt Lady Dorothy Townshend said that this hermaphrodite was the only happy couple she had ever seen.

The term 'hermaphrodite' is still used to describe people with an intersexual condition: those who are born with a body that has both male and female sexual characteristics. Consequently the word is often incorrectly used to describe transsexuals, who do not appreciate it, as they are not physically ambiguous. Since it is also quite commonly used as a term of abuse, transsexuals tend to be sensitive about it. I am probably one of the few who are enthusiastic about Hermaphroditus.

I find the idea of the hermaphrodite so appealing because it is so recognizable. Most people probably feel that they, too, are a mixture of male and female characteristics; perhaps not literally in terms of their sexual characteristics, but because they combine a masculine body with feminine behaviour, for instance. Or masculine hobbies – football! beer! – and a feminine preference for high-heeled shoes. How often do you hear women who look very feminine say in interviews that they are 'actually a boy'? Or, if they are being modest, 'half a boy'. To me, the idea of the hermaphrodite is a reminder that most people are really quite androgynous.

Literal androgyny – as an intersexual physical condition – also occurs more often than you would think. To be androgynous it is not necessary to have ambiguous genitalia. You can have other physical characteristics that do not conclusively place you in one sex or the other. Typically women have two x chromosomes (xx) and men one x and one y (xy), but approximately one in every 20,000 males has two x chromosomes, and 10 per cent of these have no y chromosome. There are women with xy chromosomes and xx women with a male gene.

There is no way in which nature exactly marks the boundary between the sexes; all kinds of combinations are possible. Pope Benedict XVI may have said that the distinction between men and women is dictated by nature, but that is simply not true. And you yourself may think that you have the body of a woman or of a man, but you do not know for certain.

On the website of the Intersex Society of North America (ISNA), I came across a chart showing statistics on different forms of intersexuality. The chart shows that one in every 1,666 people in North America is neither XX nor XY; one or two people in every 1,000 undergo surgery to 'normalize' their genitals; and one in every 100 is born with a body that differs from the standard male or female one.

How frequently does transsexuality occur?

I myself do not know what my chromosomes are. As I have not been tested, I will just assume that I have XX chromosomes: that before I started taking hormones, my body was feminine in all respects and my gender was masculine. That is why I do not consider myself intersexual but transsexual; I have moved from the feminine to the masculine domain, because that is where I feel at home.

In their 2008 article 'Transsexualism is More Common than you Think', Femke Olyslager and Lynn Conway expressed their surprise at how many people know someone who has made this transition, whereas medical publications say that only one in every 11,900 persons born as men and one in every 30,400 born as women has taken the step. How is that possible? Time to investigate.

Olyslager and Conway found that there was a substantial difference between counting the number of people who had received hormone therapy and only counting those who had undergone surgery. People who had not undergone any kind of medical treatment were often not taken into account. When Olyslager and Conway calculated the number of people who suffer from severe gender dysphoria based on the available data, they arrived at the statistic that it is one to two in every 2,000 people born as men, and one to two in every 4,000 born as women. 'We believe that these numbers are of great significance. They make the whole issue of transsexualism much less "exotic" than was often thought until now. These numbers can only improve social acceptance.'

The publication *Transgenders in the Netherlands* (2012) by the Dutch knowledge centre Rutgers WPF made transsexuality even less exotic:

According to the most recent estimate, there are more than 48,000 people living in the Netherlands who report an ambivalent or incongruent gender identity in combination with dissatisfaction about their own body and a desire for complete or partial birth sex reassignment through hormones and/or surgery. In the population aged between 15 and

70 years, this represents 0.6 per cent of men and
0.2 per cent of women.

How does it feel?

'But how does it feel?' my friend P. asked me.
    'Imagine', I said, 'that you have to go to a meet-
ing wearing a dress, and everybody calls you
madam the entire afternoon. How would you feel?'
    'Awful', he said.
    'Well,' I said, 'that's how it feels.'

Why not transcend the concept of gender?

Since I have always written about the concepts of masculinity and femininity in relative terms, I frequently get that
thrown back in my face. 'Why don't you just transcend
the division into sexes?' serious researchers and people
interested in philosophy ask me. 'Why have you taken
such a drastic step? You are a philosopher, aren't you?
Surely you could just have said that you no longer wanted
to be considered female without having to start such an
intrusive course of treatment to get a masculine body?'
    Several answers are possible here, with varying
degrees of relevance. First, I could give a very practical
answer and say yes. Of course I could approach the
whole thing philosophically. Of course I could have
stayed the way I was and have considered my female
body, on a higher level, as a male body. But if I order

a beer in a bar, it's no use me telling the waiter: 'Now listen here, I'm transcending the binary system boundaries and I consider the whole concept of gender a social construction that I'm trying to deconstruct in my performativity.' The waiter will still call me madam.

Second, I could point to social developments. In recent years, I have repeatedly drawn attention to increasing segregation. How can I single-handedly transcend the division into two sexes when society is imposing that division on me ever more rigorously? I can't fill in a form or order a cinema ticket online without having to tick the box to say whether I am a man or a woman. Of course, I might have a distorted view of reality, since I look at masculinity and femininity from an unusual perspective. But others have noticed the rising segregation too, and they oppose it just as vigorously as I do. In the week that I started to take testosterone, I read several newspaper articles warning about the increased emphasis on differences between the sexes.

In the Dutch newspaper *Het Parool*, the neurobiologist Lydia Krabbendam said: 'The more you emphasize the difference between boys and girls, the bigger it becomes.' And Dr Adam Soboczynski, the editor of the literature section of the German newspaper *Die Zeit*, complained that you cannot leave your house these days without being confronted with the difference between the sexes. Over a period of a couple of weeks he had seen what felt like a thousand television programmes focusing attention on the apparently huge difference between men and women, showing that 'sex had been raised to the main form of classification in society'. There had been programmes about how only men can pour beer properly, about the modern man's lack of masculinity, about women's moral superiority, about women's moral inferiority, and dozens about the compulsory quota of women in top business positions. His article in *Die Zeit* of 15 March 2012 bore the desperate title *'Lasst mich mit eurem Geschlecht in Ruhe!'* – Leave me in peace with your sex!

Third, I could point out that transcending the division into sexes is not the exclusive task of transsexuals. The same people who are now urging me to rise philosophically above the concepts of masculinity and femininity invited me only a year earlier to participate in women's festivals and women's debates and contribute to books full of women thinkers. Back then they apparently felt no qualms about approaching me as a woman, so let them now have no qualms about approaching me as a man. As soon as society starts attaching less importance to the sex of the individuals within it, I will be the first to welcome it, but for now I have done my duty in being compliant.

But the last answer is the best. I was and still am convinced that being a man is not the same as being very masculine (and therefore very unfeminine). Yes, I do claim that most people are androgynous, that they have a mix of feminine and masculine characteristics, and that it is therefore nonsensical to pretend that we can divide people into two kinds: women are women, men are men, and never the twain shall meet. But I do not claim that there are no men. Or that there are no women. There is really no reason at all why a philosopher with a critical attitude towards the terms 'femininity' and 'masculinity' cannot himself be a man with a desire to have a masculine body.

The inner self and the spectacle

All in all, a transition like this is a sensational event. However, this risks transsexuality being dismissed as a fad: something people do to be cool. The same used to be said of homosexuality, and it was nonsense then, too. But while you can at least experiment freely with homosexuality, transsexuality is more complicated: nobody takes such drastic social and medical steps without feeling that they are completely necessary.

Of course the physical changes are spectacular and are, for outsiders too, an interesting phenomenon to observe and think about. But the transition from one sex role to the other actually begins with shedding the pressure to be something you are not. At first that has nothing to do with physical change; only after you have relieved yourself of that obligation can you ask yourself which direction you want to go in and what you need to do to get there. Only then come the decisions about your appearance, about possible medical treatment and physical interventions. But it all starts with your inner conviction about your own identity – and the decision to live in a way that is compatible with that conviction.

two

Language and Etiquette: What You Should and Shouldn't Say

THE DAY BEFORE I started taking testosterone, a sound man was pinning a microphone on me for a radio interview. I was wearing a men's shirt and jacket. He bent towards me and said: 'I'll pin it on your blouse. Can you just move your top to one side?'

Do people actually look at each other? I sometimes wonder what they would ask J. D. Salinger on a chat show. 'Did you get drunk at the awards after-party?' Or what a shop assistant would say to Virginia Woolf: 'That would look great with stilettos.'

Grammar and gender

When I was a student, I used to spend my holidays in Israel so that I could wear work clothes for the whole summer. I regularly worked at a turkey farm, where we collected the eggs, pasteurized them and sold them to foreign countries. According to the regulations, when we arrived at the turkey sheds we first had to take a shower to prevent infection and were then given sterile clothes to wear. Strangely enough, they only had men's clothes and underwear, which discouraged many women from working there. Those who did all had their own reasons.

During one of those summers I worked with a young woman who insisted on being called Jonah, an Israeli male name, though the others usually addressed her as Joniet. One day, as she was walking past the door of a turkey shed, one of the men called out to her: 'Hey, *bachoera!*' – 'Hey, young lady!', to which she replied: '*Ani lo bachoera, ani bachoer*' – 'I am not a young lady, I am a young man.'

The fact that this response has become a standard in my repertoire of anecdotes is not only because it is so evocative. Even back then, I realized immediately that I could not borrow it, because it does not translate. In Dutch, as in English, it sounds contrived, whereas in Hebrew it sounds completely natural.

That summer, during my conversation lessons, I became aware of the opportunities that different languages offer to play with gender. The more strongly the grammar of a language emphasizes the differences between men and women, the easier it is for you to play around with it. Hebrew has four ways of saying 'I love you': *ani ohevet otach* (woman to woman), *ani ohev otach* (man to woman), *ani ohev otcha* (man to man) and *ani ohevet otcha* (woman to man). As a transgender person, that gives you something to work with.

Unlike Hebrew, Dutch or English are not very gendered: the gender of the speaker hardly influences the structure of the sentence or the form of the words. That also means that you cannot switch from one sex role to another one fine day by simply using male rather than female grammar, or vice versa. In Dutch and English, much more than in other languages, you are dependent on other people's willingness to see you in the way you want to be seen. That's not easy, because all those other people have much better things to do than pick up on the signals you are sending out. If we want to say something in Dutch or in English about our gender identity, we have to raise the subject explicitly.

Language politics: do you say 'transsexual' or 'transgender'?

Though for the time being I prefer to use the word 'transsexual' to describe my own condition, there are good reasons not to. First, it sounds as if it's about sex, which is confusing, to say the least. The same applies to the term 'homosexuality', where sex is not the main concern either: some people frequently have gay sex without ever calling themselves homosexual, and some homosexuals never have sex at all. It would be nice if you could say something about your fascinations and the romances you embark on without constantly giving the impression that you're talking about sex.

Where transsexuality is concerned, the association is even more irksome because identity has nothing to do with sex. And in English there is the added problem that 'sex' can be used to refer to the genitals, a connotation that most transsexuals find most unwelcome. Add to that the fact that the word 'transsexuality' has become emotionally charged because of a history of discrimination and social problems and you have more than enough reason to prefer the newer word 'transgender', which is much vaguer and therefore sounds nicer.

Indeed, you hear everyone dutifully saying 'gender' nowadays. One reason this term has become so widespread could be that many children have been in the news in recent years for switching sex roles. In these cases it makes sense for parents, doctors and journalists to avoid using a term that is reminiscent of sex; 'transgender' is undoubtedly better where children are concerned. And yet the word has huge drawbacks, the biggest being that no one really knows what it means.

Not only are 'trans' and 'gender' quite difficult concepts in themselves, and especially when used together, but an increasing number of people, all with different self-images, have claimed the term. They have every right to – after all, language is a living organism – but in doing so, they drag the guileless bystander along with them.

While 'transgender' was initially used as a vague euphemism for transsexuality, over time it has become a collective term for everyone who does not feel at home in the role they were assigned at birth. This includes people who have settled in the border region between the sexes; people who are fluid in their self-image; people who change role regularly or who expressly do not want to change role but do recognize themselves in the opposite sex; people who are in doubt or are searching; and sometimes also transvestites. Furthermore there is the view that transgender people are a separate third group, alongside men and women. The result of all of this is that classic transsexuals – those who have had medical treatment and then just want to get on with their lives as men or women – sometimes suddenly find themselves excluded. So they dig out the old term 'transsexuality' again, hoping that outsiders have become sufficiently enlightened to look beyond the stigma and the sexual connotations that used to be attached to it.

If I keep calling myself transsexual for the time being, it is just because I don't really know how to deal with the word 'transgender'. I'm not sure if it should be an adjective or a noun (am I transgender or *a* trans-gender?) and 'transgenderism' is a pretty clumsy term to describe the phenomenon. Although it does sound nicer than 'transsexual', it's also quite an ugly word, and I try to avoid it as much as I can. To be honest, I hope that at some time in the not too distant future, I will no longer have to describe myself in terms like these at all: that I will have put this whole episode behind me and will be able to live without having to explain myself. A man with a past.

Cis, trans and alphabet soup

When you look for words to talk about sex change, you will find yourself in a world with a jargon all of its own in which everyone who is not 'trans' is 'cis'. In Latin *cis* means 'on this side of', and is opposed to *trans* ('on or to the other side of'). People who feel that their identity matches the sex they were born with are cis. So besides transmen and transwomen there are cis men and cis women. And there is a cis community of people who are cis gender, and of course have something like cis identity or cis awareness.

A cis man is also simply called a born man, or a bio man (though this is controversial, as it implies that a transman is not 'bio', which raises the question of how he functions). If you want to be absolutely sure that you don't make a blunder, just stick to the factual description and refer to people as 'born XY' or 'born XX' – though you will have to ask the person concerned for that medical information beforehand.

There is also a big difference between people who are 'binary identified' and those who are 'non-binary identified'. The word binary indicates a division: people adhering to the binary system divide humankind into women and men. Those who do not think in binary terms jettison the old dichotomy and assume that each individual has entirely their own – perhaps even unique – gender identity, a personal combination of characteristics and traits. Anyone who first calls themselves a man and then, after the transition, a woman is complying with the binary system; many transgenders, however, reject this division.

All this terminology is intended to make it easier to talk about transsexuality. You can only explain properly that you may not want to be a man any longer, but neither do you want to be a woman, if you have terms like 'transgender' and 'binary system' to back you up. Furthermore for political purposes it is absolutely necessary to create an idiom that enables you to stand up for your rights and defend your interests. Anyone who wishes to draw attention to the position of a certain group in society must first be able to identify them by name.

That is why we should welcome the fact that identity is being talked about with increasing precision. In the last twenty years a great deal of progress has been made in acknowledging mutual differences. In the 1990s, after much deep thought, the initial collective term LGB – lesbian, gay, bisexual – expanded to become LGBTT2IQ: lesbian, gay, bisexual, transgender, transsexual, two-spirited, intersexual, queer. Everyone who subsequently wanted to add their own flavour to this alphabet soup could toss in letters to their own taste, from C for 'curious' to U for 'uncertain'.

The danger of this precision is that it will lead to such a degree of fragmentation that ultimately each individual will be in their own unique group. You occasionally see this in schisms in churches and political parties and it rarely testifies to flexibility or a great talent for solidarity. It is good to be aware that we all have our own unique gender identities, but that does not mean that we should all end up forming our own separate categories.

Inappropriate questions

In America, where they are more sensitive than we are over here, some people keep a sharp look out for expressions of 'cissexism': that is, the conviction that the gender of a transsexual has less value or is less authentic than that of a cissexual. Anyone afraid of being cissexist should bear in mind that most transgender people have spent so much time reflecting on human shortcomings that they have become unusually tolerant and will not easily take offence at what others say. Yet a few questions are seriously inappropriate for cis people to ask when they are talking to a transwoman or transman.

What is your real name?
Your new name is your real name now. The name your parents chose for you was no more real. Not from a philosophical point of view, nor in practice.

Have you had surgery yet?
Surgical operations – and this cannot be said often enough – are of no relevance to the outside world. The only changes that are important for a successful social transition are those that change what other people see: clothing, presentation and the visible effects of hormone therapy. Any surgery that does occur just makes a few

adjustments to the body underneath the clothes and is therefore only relevant to the person concerned and those they share a bed with. Asking someone about 'the operation' amounts to asking them about their genitals. Is that decent? What did your mother teach you about asking embarrassing questions?

How do you have sex?
Since my transition, journalists whom I don't know from Adam have called me up to ask about my sex life. Do I still have sex? And how? Do people still want to have sex with me? Let me make this clear: every question you wouldn't ask any other guest on a talk show ('How big is yours? Is your wife happy with it?'), you don't ask a trans-sexual guest either. In the 1950s the famous transwoman Christine Jorgensen was once asked by a journalist: 'Are the historic parts you had removed stored someplace?'

Inappropriate terms

(S)he
I'm not easily offended, but I did once get severely riled when I read an article by a serious journalist who wanted to know if I am 'a (s)he'. What she meant to ask was whether I am intersexual: that is, whether my body is literally so ambiguous that I am neither man nor woman. Apart from the fact that that is a pretty rude question in itself, it was her use of the term 'a (s)he' that really got my back up.

The journalist undoubtedly wanted to show me that she was well-informed and knew the jargon. But that kind of jargon is deceptive. If you start experimenting with it against the express wishes of those concerned, you will soon start making painful faux pas. People can present themselves as '(s)he', but if someone calls himself 'he', why would you say '(s)he' or even worse, 'a (s)he'?

She/he
Slightly less objectionable, but still unacceptable, as it suggests that you have suddenly become two people.

Transsexual man
If you mean a woman: a male-to-female transsexual is a woman. A female-to-male transsexual is a man. And thus the excellent documentary *I Am a Woman Now* (2011) by Dutch filmmaker Michiel van Erp about women who had been operated on by Dr Georges Burou in Casablanca was not about 'transsexual men', as several self-respecting voices in the media stated, but about transsexual women.

A transsexual too
As in: 'A friend of mine is a transsexual, too.' This isn't so bad, but it is strange simply to dismiss a friend as part of a category, especially with no further explanation. I recognized this bluntness from my homosexual period. Someone would nudge me and say 'You're a lesbian, aren't you?' When I said yes, they would add: 'A friend of mine is a lesbian, too.' And that was it. Full stop. Silence.

Yes, transsexuals are very nice people
If meant as something kind to say to you personally.
This implies that you are not a human being but a
species. Like when you look affectionately at a little
dog running around in the park and its owner says:
'Yes, they're very lively.'

Nonpliments

And then, to make everyone even more nervous about
talking to transsexuals, there are the 'nonpliments', things
intended as a compliment but that have completely the
opposite effect. Like: 'Wow, you look just like a real
man.' Or: 'You used to be such a nice woman.' And the
one that bluntly exposes the most indelible prejudice of
all: 'You look better than all those other transsexuals.'

 The most subtle expression of condescension I have
experienced came in an email message from a distant
acquaintance, which showed me how pitiful my situation
had become. He apparently had an image of me roaming
the streets as an outcast. 'Don't forget,' he said, 'you can
always call on us.'

Etiquette

After this rather grim catalogue of things that can go
wrong in communications with transsexuals, I hasten
to say that most of the time people are fine and have
no trouble with it at all. That is because of their innate

good nature, or perhaps because they tend to be more concerned with themselves than with others.

When I was young, I always used to swim in a pair of trunks and a T-shirt. Once, in a small lake somewhere in France, I attracted the attention of an eight-year-old boy who looked at me, bewildered, and shouted 'Look, *maman*, that lady is swimming in a T-shirt.' His mother gave me an indifferent look and said: '*C'est son problème*' (That's her problem). And indeed it was.

This laconic approach is the basis of etiquette. Everyone has their own problems and it is unbecoming to pass severe judgement on them or make harsh statements about them. If a transman swims in a T-shirt, or a trans-woman in a bathing suit, it is his or her business, and if polite outsiders happen to notice, they should pretend not to. In their turn polite transsexuals don't demand that all their neighbours and acquaintances immediately drop what they are doing and start immersing themselves full-time in the ins and outs of their transition. In the writings of American activists I sometimes see cisgendered compatriots being urged to do all kinds of things: become aware, study, be sympathetic, show solidarity, express their opinions and man the barricades. As if they have nothing better to do.

We all have our problems. It would save a lot of irritation all round if people would become aware of that; if one group would realize that those in another group are busy enough leading their own lives and coping with their own issues. One might be undergoing difficult IVF treatment in an attempt to become pregnant, while another is struggling with gambling debts; someone else might have an adolescent daughter who has fallen under the spell of a pimp, while others are faced with illness, family feuds, depression and other problems they do not want to talk about. Your gender – or it may be your colour, or your religion – can be all-decisive in the way your life goes to an extent that other people cannot begin to imagine. On a discussion site, a young transman rightfully sighed: 'Someone's gotta live it, might as well be us.'

The rules of conduct

Despite all these qualifications, there are two rules of conduct I would recommend when dealing with transsexuals, based on the idea that if you can make each other's lives easier, you should certainly not miss the opportunity.

Accept that people belong to the gender they say they belong to
If someone announces his transition, saying that from now on he is going to live as a man and would like to be addressed accordingly, you should say 'he' and use his new name. Of course you might slip up – but you should do your best.

No matter how simple and obvious this change to 'he' is, I have noticed that some people categorically refuse to go along with it. They stick doggedly to 'she' and 'her' because they think they are the only ones clever enough to know that you are fooling everybody. Usually these are people who are very content with the share they were allocated when intelligence was being handed out. Like the old man from the countryside who said on television that he knew that people had never walked on the Moon, they know that really you are still a woman. After giving this attitude a lot of thought, I have concluded that it is stupidity, not impoliteness, and so there is nothing to be done about it.

Don't talk to others about someone else's transition
No one needs to know that the man standing in front of them used to live as a woman. Gossiping is a useful and pleasant way of passing the time, but gossiping about someone's sex change is not without its dangers. 'Outing' can have unpleasant consequences for someone's job or for their social and family relationships.

Even if someone is completely open about their situation, that still does not give you the right to 'out' them to others. Sometimes a transman can be open about his past in one situation but not in another. It is up to him to decide when he wants to talk about his transition, not you.

three

Rules and Laws

IN THE SUMMER of 2012, without a hint of resistance, Argentina adopted Law 26,743. The bill received the unanimous support of the Senate. Since the new law came into force, transsexuals have been able to have their sex changed in the official records at their own initiative without a doctor's diagnosis or the approval of a judge. No questions are asked about operations or medical treatment: their own conviction is sufficient. This 'Gender Identity' Law makes Argentina the first country in the world where a person's body no longer plays a role in the registration of their sex.

Around the world governments are looking for ways to make it easier for people to change their sex officially. Spain and Britain, for example, have introduced new laws in recent years, but these countries require at least an expert diagnosis of persistent gender dysphoria. By abandoning this requirement, Argentina has taken a revolutionary step forward. Law 26,743 returns the right of self-determination to citizens: they can determine their gender identity themselves and have it registered in their official records. If you no longer want to be registered as a man but as a woman, you simply tell the authorities that this has been a long-standing wish, and ten days later the change is complete.

'There is nothing new under the sun', said Argentine president Cristina Fernández de Kirchner at the ceremony to issue the first identity papers to transsexuals. 'None of the things we now recognize in law are new. They are part of the history of humankind and it is time to accept that reality is not as we wish it, or as others wish it – reality is as it is.'

The law in Europe

The Netherlands has long suffered the disadvantages of being a pioneer in the field of transsexuality. It was one of the first countries to enable individuals to change their sex in official records. And, together with other pioneers like Sweden and Germany, it was stuck with obsolete laws. Apparently it was still taken for granted in the 1980s that sterilization should be included in law as a requirement. Anyone wishing to change their sex in official records came up against strict conditions: your body had to be fully modified to the desired sex and you had to be unable to father or give birth to children. As a consequence people were forced to undergo medical treatment that they did not want. If they wanted to obtain the right official papers, they had no other choice than to accept the government's demands.

These cruel and inhumane criteria attracted the attention of the Council of Europe and the UN Commission on Women's Rights, and in 2011 Human Rights Watch published a report on the situation, entitled 'Controlling Bodies, Denying Identities'. Later that same year the Dutch government initiated changes to the law, to ban the forced sterilization of transsexual people. This came into force in July 2014. In Sweden a court ruled in 2012 that compulsory sterilization was contrary to the Swedish Constitution and the European Convention on Human Rights. As a result of this ruling, the law was revised and in 2013 the sterilization requirement was scrapped.

Sterilization is not a requirement in Britain. Until recently, however, you faced the complication that you had to end your marriage if you wanted to legally change your gender. This was to avoid couples ending up in same-sex marriages, which until recently were not permitted in the UK. Since same-sex marriages are now legal, this is no longer a problem.

Under the new Dutch legislation, a sustained conviction of belonging to the other sex is sufficient to get the official records changed. As an 'expert' opinion is still required, the Netherlands remains behind Argentina in this respect. But it is certainly a step in the right direction. And once the changes come into force, the government will no longer be able to harass individuals about operations.

Clothing

The rules are also changing for the better at a more local level. In the summer of 2012 the university magazine *The Oxford Student* announced that all references to gender would be removed from the university's dress code and that students were therefore no longer obliged to wear clothing considered appropriate to their official gender during examinations. In other words, women no longer had to wear a skirt and tights or stockings when they took an exam. This modification of the traditional dress code was intended especially to meet the needs of transgender students.

Consequently male students at Oxford can now turn up for exams in a skirt and tights, and female students in a suit and tie. The dress code still applies, the traditions continue to be honoured, but it is recognized that some students consider themselves members of the opposite sex, or rather, not to belong to the gender allocated to them.

The matter was raised by the Lesbian, Gay, Bisexual, Trans and Queer Society at the university. In the past, if students were not able or willing to comply with the strict dress code, they had to apply for formal dispensation from their university proctor. For those who found the prospect of facing this fearsome figure too daunting, the obligation to wear clothing they despised added to their pre-exam jitters. Either way they were assured of extra agitation. The LGBTQ Society was pleased to announce that the slight change in the rules had resulted in the exams being 'significantly less stressful'.

Sport

In the field of sport the rules are also changing. The International Olympic Committee (IOC) has admitted transsexual women to women's events since the 2004 Athens games. There are, however, a number of conditions attached. Transwomen have to wait for a number of years after the transition to ensure that they do not have an unfair advantage from any remnants of their masculinity. Banning such 'advantages' is however the subject of heated debate. Some argue that genetic and hormonal advantages are at the core of competition in sport. If everyone were the same, there would be no point in holding sporting events.

In the past there have been considerable controversies about the sex of athletes. These usually focused on the suspicion that a female athlete was in fact a man, or at least had so many male characteristics that she could no longer be considered a woman according to the rules of the competition. The authorities were not very sensitive in dealing with such cases. Harsh accusations were made in public about women who had been completely unaware of their intersexuality until that moment. And the affairs tended to run on endlessly.

One notorious case in the Netherlands was that of Foekje Dillema (1926–2007), a top athlete and the great rival of multiple Olympic gold-medallist Fanny Blankers-Koen. Prior to the 1950 European Championships, the International Association of Athletics Federations required all female athletes to take a sex test. According to Dillema's biographer Max Dohle, the reason for the tests was given, rather charmingly, as 'to exclude deceivers and hermaphrodites' from the competition. Because she was unwilling to take the test, Dillema was suspended for life. She refused ever to speak about the affair again. After her death the Dutch Athletics Union offered their apologies to her family for the insensitive way in which she had been expelled from the sport.

Today, too, intersexuals – people with both male and female characteristics – suffer more from conditions and regulations in sport than transsexuals. Sometimes athletics federations or the IOC decide to stop conducting sex tests, but as soon as women start to perform at levels that men find exceptional – as happened with Caster Semenya in 2009 – the tests are reintroduced. Because it is difficult to determine whether someone is a woman or a man – there are so many criteria and they all produce different results – the rules are continually changing. At present the main focus is on the level of testosterone in the blood of an athlete and whether her body responds to the hormone.

For transsexuals the rules are clearer. In a recommendation to sports clubs and federations, the Dutch Olympic Committee states that it supports the participation of transgender people in competitions of the gender of their preference. In the words of the Committee, 'if the sex change has been completed fully – that is, there has been a minimum of three years of hormone treatment, or if the person concerned has registered their new sex in the official records and/or has undergone a sex-change operation – there is no reason why they should not take part in the competition for their new sex.' Still complicated, but clear nevertheless.

Privacy

If you don't have a problem with something, it is often difficult to imagine that it might be a problem for some-one else. How bad can it be having to wear a skirt and tights during an exam? When the full-body scanner was introduced at airports, there was widespread agreement that privacy should take second place to security. How bad was it to be seen naked in front of one or two secur-ity officers? 'After all, if you've nothing to hide . . .'.

But everyone has something to hide. In the case of the body scanner, it is primarily people with diseases, missing limbs and other physical disabilities that become aware of this. Shortly after the scanners were introduced, concerned transsexual men asked each other what they should do if they were forced to enter the machine. One young man related with relish that after being scanned, he had been asked what he was hiding in his underwear. With his whole family watching, he opened his trousers, pulled out a plastic penis and slapped it down on the table. The shocked security officers immediately gave him permission to go on his way.

After an experimental period, it was decided not to permit the use of full-body scans at airports in Europe – not because of the far-reaching invasion of human dignity but because the radiation proved to be carcinogenic. 'Well, in that case . . .,' I hear you say, 'that's different.'

Unnecessary display of sex

Modern science and technology seem to have made gender transition easier, especially if laws are also updated. But there were times when changing your gender was considerably easier than it is now – not officially or legally, but in practice. I have always looked at nineteenth-century literature, which abounds in transitions and metamorphoses, with a certain degree of envy. Some of the books describe cases of mistaken identity; others tell of people who left their old lives behind them to start completely afresh elsewhere. Our ancestors were fascinated by uncertain identities, by disguises and doubles. Take the popular doppelgänger motif, or the twin motif in ancient folk cultures and modern soap operas. The emerging twin brother, the lost son, the mask of Zorro, the Count of Monte Cristo, the wolf in the guise of the old grandmother, *The Importance of Being Earnest*, the frog who turns out to be a prince,

Les Misérables. All strangers and loners trying to escape their fate through metamorphosis.

Compared to a past when women could 'prove the prettier fellow of the two, and wear [their] dagger with the braver grace', as Shakespeare wrote in *The Merchant of Venice*, it is now considerably more difficult to take on a different gender role. These days, pretty fellows who are not what they seem are immediately exposed on the basis of their telephone data or the fingerprints in their passport, which are stored in a central database. Our identities are strictly checked by all kinds of external authorities: we are examined, measured, registered, bugged and diagnosed, and every characteristic of our bodies is carried off in a test tube so we can be told whether we are male or female.

At a time when DNA testing had not yet been developed, Foekje Dillema would have won the European Championships as a woman. But she was suspended and, after her death, skin cells were removed from her clothing and checked for gender characteristics in a university laboratory. The results were announced to the people of the Netherlands through the public media. Why? Because there is a rule that bans women with a Y chromosome from competing in sporting events.

Yes, we do now have a law that makes it possible to change your sex in the official records. But at the same time we have introduced all kinds of new rules that smoke transgender people out from their hiding places. Not only do you have to state your sex much more frequently and emphatically than before – many digital forms cannot be filled in unless you tick the male/ female box – but many organizations know your sex already because they share their databases. In addition more and more data are known that provide information on our biological make-up.

That makes the wild, romantic nineteenth-century literature even more seductive. In novels from the era before modern technology, you can read of people who started their lives anew after experiencing misfortune by taking on another identity. This freedom to transform who you are has disappeared in our modern age. It is therefore time to reclaim something of that freedom by creating more liberal possibilities to change one's sex.

four

Body

CHANGING YOUR BODY: it's not only transsexuals who do it. There are born women who undergo surgery to feel more feminine, born men who take male hormones to become more masculine. In a certain sense they, too, are in transition. Clearly they feel that something is wrong with their level of femininity or masculinity, and they want to do something about it. As the American comedian Ian Harvie says, 'Dolly Parton is trans, Kenny Rogers is trans. All these people who've have had this work done: they're so trans and they just don't even know it.'

Harvie has a point. You could indeed say that the phrase 'born in the wrong body' does not apply exclusively to people who make the transition from man to woman or vice versa. Hardly anyone has a body that fits them perfectly. We mainly harp on about 'the wrong body' in relation to transsexuality as an easy way out. It sounds pathetic and harmless, making the transition digestible. And it means that others no longer have to struggle with their own masculinity or femininity – after all, they are normal and were born in the right body.

In reality it is a superficial way of lumping together all the widely varying feelings and individual life stories of people who experience gender discomfort – a 'soundbite of struggle', as I once read. In Ian Harvie's words: 'I usually just say that so that people who aren't that fucking bright can also understand it.'

The wrong body

Contrary to what the 'soundbite of struggle' suggests, gender dysphoria can take a wide variety of forms. I know of people who mainly need an urgent boost from the right hormones. As soon as the testosterone or oestrogen starts flowing through their body, they feel like a new person. Others don't recognize their own bodies, or can't look at themselves in the mirror because they can't bear the sight of their sexual characteristics.

For me, the sight of my own body was never the main problem; rather, it was the embarrassment it caused me out in the big, wide world. These feelings are hard to explain; let me just say that shame was the key problem, not so much because my body appeared strange to me, but because of the signals it sent out, causing others to see me as a woman. I was embarrassed to be seen in a way in which I didn't want to be seen. It can perhaps best be compared to those adolescent night-mares where you are walking naked through the crowded corridors of your school to fetch your clothes, which for some strange reason are on your French teacher's desk.

It is not that the panic literally had to do with being naked, but it was that same desperate feeling of being exposed to the stares of the people around you without having any influence on what they thought of you.

Outsiders often think that transsexuals mainly want to have their genitals modified, but they play the least significant role in how people assign femininity: nobody sees them when you go into a baker's to buy a loaf of bread. So the fact that panic could strike in a baker's, during a lecture, when opening my mail and in all social situations in which I was addressed as a woman had much more to do with the signals sent out by my voice, my face, my posture, my name and, all in all, with the social role I had been assigned on the basis of all those signals. It was not my body as such, but my body as an interface for my contact with the outside world that stood in my way.

Having said that, I immediately have to contradict myself. Of course I would also look at my body in the mirror at times, puzzled, but not always with disgust or revulsion. 'You're fighting your incarnation', I was once told by a doctor I visited as a 28-year-old because I was suffering from fatigue, and she was right.

Objectively it was not the wrong body, but it didn't look like me. It just wasn't me. Largely in order to look more boyish I had, in the years before I went to the doctor, lost more weight than was sensible, which had caused the fatigue. And once I had put on some weight I would start fighting my incarnation again. My clothes did not hang as

I wanted them to, the lines were too soft, my voice was too feminine. I might not have been incarnated at birth as a dung beetle or the monstrous '*Ungeziefer*' described by Franz Kafka in *The Metamorphosis*, but I had been born with a body whose nuances I did not understand.

Spending my life writing was not a bad makeshift solution. It allowed me to take part in discussions without being 'incarnated' – without those I was talking to continually being reminded of which sex I had been born into – until the outside world locked me up in the internment camp of female writers and thinkers, that is. I then realized that all that writing had got me nowhere at all.

The right body

Almost no one seems to know this, but taking male hormones really does change your body into a man's. Nobody knows because from the outside you can't see all the effects at a single glance. What's more, a slightly built and introvert philosopher doesn't suddenly change into a broad-shouldered lumberjack – he simply remains a slightly built and introvert philosopher. But hormonally – chemically – he is no longer female and the male hormones affect every aspect of his body. That is the most amazing aspect of the transition: that you do change and don't change at the same time.

When people around you decide to prepare themselves for your big step, they sometimes imagine that you will get a completely new and improved body. Some even think that you will get a new personality, with new hobbies, talents and moods. These are the people who, when they first see you, note with surprise and a certain disappointment that not that much has really changed. And you do indeed stay the same: you still live in your own body and your dog doesn't suddenly see you as a stranger.

But at the same time, the testosterone changes your body at such a pace that it can scare you. I have seen young men who stop after three months (which is not advisable from a medical viewpoint) and resume a little later. From American films on YouTube I also know that people sometimes stop permanently after a while because they are becoming more masculine than they feel is wise.

On Friday 10 August 2012 – almost five months after I had started taking testosterone – my body became masculine in the eyes of the outside world. The day before, while shopping in the village, I had still been addressed as 'madam', but on this particular Friday I entered a shop in a neighbouring village and was greeted with 'sir'. I immediately went to the next shop to see if it was a one-off, but the shop assistant there showed no sign of hesitation, so I went on to the next shop, and then to the snack bar and the petrol station, and apparently everywhere I went they saw a man coming in.

What had changed? In the intervening 24 hours I hadn't been to the hairdresser's and I wasn't wearing different clothes; the testosterone had just slightly changed the subtle signals with which my body suggests its sex. It must have been something in the lines of my face, or in the relation of my shoulders to my hips. Whatever it was, between one moment and the next I had crossed the line for good.

Ever since that day in August, my body has been functioning as a male body in the company of strangers without giving me too much trouble. 'Looks like a man and behaves like a man', is what the judge said in reply to my request to change my first name. I don't actually know how a man behaves, nor am I trying particularly hard to do so, but in any case it was sufficient for my name to be changed. In the months that followed there was the occasional minor relapse when someone would hesitate for a moment and guess wrongly, but on the whole strangers have mistaken my sex only on very rare occasions. There was a time in the autumn of 2012, which only counts as half, when a boy at the till in the super-market accidentally called me both 'madam' and 'sir'. He felt so embarrassed by his own confusion that he gave me some extra stickers for my children, in the event that I had any children.

That was the start of a complicated double life. While strangers see a man in my body, it is very different among people I know. Their old image of me is still so powerful that they cannot see the new one. And if not that, it is the forms of address, the pronouns, that have been engraved in their brains with such sharp needles that they can only perceive me in female terms. Changing my first name is something most of them can handle, but saying 'he' proves to be almost impossible.

While I perfectly understand this, and am willing to wait patiently for the old image to fade and for people to become used to saying 'he', I do get seriously concerned when I notice that people still use female words to refer to men who underwent their transition ten years ago. When a renowned sociologist uses 'he' to refer to the economist Deirdre McCloskey in a serious newspaper, he clearly does not understand what it means that McCloskey is a woman.

Among intellectuals in particular, the misconception persists that a sex change is something abstract: a social construction or deconstruction of gender, an academic play of identities, very interesting as long as you are debating the subject, but in daily life not much more than dressing up. Apparently they don't realize that with hormones, you can quite easily cross the vague border between femininity and masculinity – not in an abstract sense, not as an intellectual pretence, but for real. Your body changes – its chemistry, its structure, its software and hardware – until you feel that you no longer inhabit a female but a male body. Once again that happened to me quite unexpectedly: one fine day I realized I was walking around in the body of a man. Don't ask me to describe this self-perception. That's just the way it was. The feelings of ridiculousness and failure had gone.

Of course I am physically still a combination of male and female characteristics – just like everyone else. The human body is a varied patchwork of deviations from the norm. Your brain structure may be more feminine than your legs. You may be sending out such mixed signals that the boys on the till at the supermarket get confused. Or you may be Dolly Parton and feel the desire to bump up your femininity a little more. That's why I am surprised when I hear a transsexual compliantly admit to an interviewer that she is not 'a real woman'. Why not? Because she has a male past? I listen to all this talk about real women and real men with scepticism. Show me a real man and I will immediately admit that I am not one.

Passing as a man: from Norah to Ned

Women sometimes say to me proudly that they could easily pass as a man. To which I say: I'm sure you could. Putting on different clothes and talking a little more gruffly will get you a long way.

The American columnist Norah Vincent did exactly that and wrote a book about it. I her book *Self-made Man: One Woman's Year Disguised as a Man*, Vincent describes how she went undercover as a man for a year and a half, visited monasteries and strip clubs and joined a bowling league. Vincent went about the project professionally, changing more than just her clothes. To transform herself from Norah into Ned, she enlisted the help of a make-up artist who gave her a five o'clock shadow and had months of training from a Juilliard voice coach. Perhaps she needed all that professional help, because she was not really a man, nor did she become one: she only dressed up as one for the purposes of her book.

Vincent did very well 'passing as a man': she was not unmasked once in the whole eighteen months and integrated fully with groups of men as a man. But the project was a failure in a different way: it was *being* a man that she found so difficult. After hearing herself being referred to as 'him' and 'Ned' for a year and a half, she sank into a deep depression and even had to be admitted to a psychiatric clinic.

Identity, she concluded, was not something you should play around with. 'When you mess around with that, you really mess around with something that you need that helps you to function', she said in an interview with ABC *News*. 'And I found out that gender lives in your brain and is something much more than costume. And I really learned that the hard way.' She added that she was healed now and was glad to be rid of Ned.

What physical changes do hormones cause?

Transsexuality is not a competition about who looks the most masculine. That is one conclusion you could draw from Vincent's experiment. It is not about passing for a man with the aid of stubble and a voice coach. It is about confirming your identity. That does not necessarily require far-reaching physical changes: some men succeed very well in getting their masculinity acknowledged without medical treatment. But most transmen definitely do need testosterone, if only because they want to finally recognize their bodies as their own.

Let me repeat: if you do decide to take testosterone, you should not underestimate its effects. It will take you to completely different regions of maleness/masculinity, both inside and outside, invisible and visible. If you are not completely certain, you should be extremely careful. As Vincent learned, identity is not something you should mess around with. When I hear that female doctors sometimes take a lick of testosterone the night before a conference so that they will make a stronger impression, my hair stands on end.

Anyone who does decide, after sufficient consideration, to take the male hormone will experience the following weird and wonderful changes.

Age

Before long you become a mere stripling. People in their thirties who have started hormone treatment complain about being taken for schoolboys, or the sons of their girlfriends. When I started giving lectures again after having lain low for a couple of months, I got surprised reactions: 'Sir, can I ask you something? You look so young. But when I look at your cv, you must be nearing forty.' After taking testosterone for a couple of years, you will automatically become a little older again. At least, I hope so.

Adam's apple

The younger of my two granddaughters, who are biologically my girlfriend's granddaughters, asked a good question when I informed them of my plans: 'Will you get an Adam's apple?' This is apparently an important issue to an eight-year-old. Yes, I said, some people get an Adam's apple after taking testosterone for a long time. And others don't. Adam's apples tend to vary widely in size generally, and that applies as much to new men as to born men.

Body hair

There is a funny interview on YouTube with the famous French photographer Bettina Rheims, who has been photographing androgynous models for quite some time and has had exhibitions in Düsseldorf, Berlin and Paris with her project *Gender Studies*. The exhibitions featured portraits of transgender people, about whom – as became clear from the interview – she understands refreshingly little. She had met, for the first time, men who had been born as women, and the encounters had left a great impression on her. Why are these people not as happy as she is with their femininity? she asks in surprise. And how emotional it had been to witness the horrible pain of the transformation – 'that they had to grow hair all over the place!'

I don't think most men suffer terribly from all that hair growing everywhere. What is more, not everyone grows hair all over their bodies when they take testosterone: it varies widely. Some say that they look like werewolves after only three months, while others show no traces of body hair at all after several years. Rheims must have taken enough pictures of born men to know that many of them also have little body hair. It's mainly a matter of genes.

Libido

No matter how old you are, as soon as you start taking testosterone, you hit puberty. This has several unpleasant effects: you get bored, you are hardly interested in the worries of the grown-up world, you are easily irritated and your libido soars to unreasonable heights.

On the websites of bodybuilders I have read that men who are born as men and who use testosterone gel to make their muscles grow sometimes rub some of the gel on their unsuspecting wives for this last reason. This would be a smart trick if the effects of testosterone were limited to increasing the libido, but I hope that a lot of bodybuilders don't now have wives with an Adam's apple, body hair and a masculine self-image.

In the course of time, by the way, the libido falls back to acceptable levels. The extent to which it rises and falls also differs from one person to another.

Hair loss

Going bald is a sensitive issue for all men. Taking testosterone can make you go bald. Not everyone, but it's possible. A couple of months after you've started taking hormones, your hair will thin out at the temples, and in many cases it will fall out in big clumps. This is the point at which everyone gets a shock, no matter how well-prepared they are, and when some of those who set out on the adventure for the thrill of it give up altogether.

Yet this loss of hair is the first sign not of baldness but of a change in the hairline, which is different in men and women. The sideburns will start to grow and after a while the hairline on either side of the forehead will recede a little more: this is not a sign that the end is near, either.

Going bald will happen later. Or not, I hasten to add, just to reassure myself. Again, just like the ability to grow a moustache or a beard, it is a matter of genes and predisposition.

Type

I don't know why, but in some strange way I have become more conservative in appearance. It's probably not so much because women look less conservative than men, more because something conservative inside of me was waiting to be liberated.

Skin

There are women who would prefer to be a bit more muscular and have a slightly lower voice, not to mention a different fat distribution. The temptation to take testosterone can be strong. But all those women who want to remain women should realize that taking testosterone will certainly not make them more attractive. Your skin gets coarser and puberty brings acne. Some men suffer from very severe acne during their transition, and fighting it is a much-discussed topic on forums.

Muscle power

It is remarkable how much your muscle power increases when you take testosterone. 'That lack of strength, isn't that just women being theatrical?' men ask me when I tell them this. No, they are not being theatrical. Every object that previously I could barely lift, I now just pick up and put down again a few metres away without the slightest effort. Even when you've hardly started taking testosterone, you'll see how your body has got stronger and in the mirror you'll suddenly notice muscles you didn't know you had.

Ears

In the film *Albert Nobbs* (2011), Glenn Close played the role of a woman who poses as a man so as to be able to keep working. Close wanted to play Albert so much that she invested her own money in the film. After dressing and being transformed into a man by makeup artists, she became very emotional when she saw herself in the mirror, saying, 'I cried when I first saw myself as a man.'

'Working on the look of Albert was a very long process,' Close explained, 'because the one thing we always knew is it's not about putting on a moustache or doing anything other than trying to figure out how that life would change your face.'

Close was fitted with a wig, a bigger nose and bigger ears. It was the ears in particular that left a big impression on me. Until then I had never thought about it, but I now know that a 'real man' has very large ears.

Voice

Testosterone will make your voice deeper. It will start to croak and then break. After only a couple of weeks it will ruin your singing voice, and you should count yourself lucky if you ever learn to sing again.

Nowadays people on the telephone generally guess what sex I am. And as I definitely don't want to reveal my past to every outsider, that can sometimes lead to strange conversations.

'Hello?'

'Good afternoon, sir, can I speak to Marjolijn Februari?'

'No,' I reply. 'She's not here. Can I take a message?'

'We have a cheap insurance offer for her.'

'Ah, very nice. But she's not interested.'

'Are you sure?'

'Absolutely. We've discussed it at length.'

'Maybe you could suggest it to her again?'

'Will do. While we're sitting together on the settee this evening.'

'Thank you very much. Goodbye, sir.'

Posture

I have always suffered from having a waist. But the testosterone soon started to do its work here, too. My metabolism increased slightly, the fat was distributed around my body in a different way and some of it turned into muscle. I became straighter and more sinewy. And because my shoulders had become broader, within a couple of months I had to buy my jackets two sizes bigger. Trousers, on the other hand, had to be one or two sizes smaller.

Peeing standing up

The King James Bible describes man as he 'that pisseth against the wall' (1 Samuel 25:22; 25:34; 1 Kings 14:10; 16:11; 21:21; 2 Kings 9:8). The connection between masculinity and peeing standing up goes back a long way, but it remains a point of contention. Doctors claim that sitting down is healthier for the bladder and prostate, political parties all over the world urge that peeing standing up should be banned because it is unhygienic, heated theological discussions take place about God's views on standing up or sitting down – and there isn't a woman in the world who wouldn't like just once to pee against a tree.

The transsexual man who moves from the ladies' to the men's room has a number of options. If he wants to pee standing up, he can have surgery to make that possible, or he could try a 'urination funnel', those devices used by women at music festivals and other big events, though they require practice and an imperturbable disposition. Or he could follow the advice of doctors and politicians and pee sitting down, just like other sensible men.

Penis

Okay, the time has come: we have to talk about the penis. You would be surprised at how many civilized and highly educated people start bluntly talking to me about penises at a reception over a cup of tea. Sometimes they make a special effort to come over to me to tell me that they don't want to talk about my transition, because it is very normal, a transition like this, nothing to feel awkward about, totally unnecessary. After we've shared a few moments together of staring at the floor in profound silence, they will suddenly look up and ask: 'Do you want a penis?' As if they have a spare one that they want to get rid of.

This question about my genitals is quite understandable, but not very good manners. Other men never get asked about their penises. We don't know whether most of the men we encounter in public have one or not. Newsreaders? Politicians? Managers? No idea. Yes, ballet dancers have one. But strangely enough, they don't have a masculine image.

As I said, this fascination with genitals is understandable, not only because of the sexual connotations but also because when a child is born, the genitals are the only visible individual aspect. Other than that, there is little we can discover about a newborn baby. But we do not stay babies for the rest of our lives. The more our personality rises to the surface, the clearer our gender expression becomes and the less relevant our genitals become to the outside world. This is why adults rarely ask each other about them in public. Penises, in short, are of no importance at a reception.

Let me be kind enough to explain, once and for all, about transsexual men and their penises. Clearly people are concerned, and there is really no need to be.

People would be less concerned if they knew that testosterone causes genital growth, namely of the sexual organ the transsexual man was born with. To the extent, in fact, that a transman is unlikely to feel that he has no penis.

Over time I have followed the reports of many men on their transitions and I've noticed that they all tend to follow a set format reminiscent of Bridget Jones's diary. Like Bridget, who starts each entry with an exact listing of how many alcohol units ('14'), cigarettes ('22') and calories ('5,424') she has consumed, and how much weight she has gained as a result, transmen report at regular intervals on how much their voice has dropped, how spectacularly their biceps have grown and how much they have grown 'down below', as it is discreetly referred to by all concerned.

Should a man still wish for more, a variety of surgical procedures are available to make it all look more like the organ of a born man. There are a lot of options, ranging from a simple extension to a full realistic reconstruction. The most radical surgery is still at an experimental stage and, because it cannot guarantee that you will retain your erotic sensitivity, by no means all men go for such a deluxe model. I don't hear much regret in the reports

– most men are sufficiently assured of their masculinity without it.

In the end everybody should decide for themselves if size matters. In some countries you need a penis to have your sex changed in the official records, but none of them actually specify legally how long the thing has to be, either.

Okay, so what were we talking about? Oh, yes. My penis. Do I want a penis, do I have a penis, what kind of penis, questions, questions, questions. Well, next time we meet in the foyer of a concert hall, feel free to raise the subject, but I'm afraid you'll never get an answer.

five

Society: The Tensions Surrounding the Transition

AFTER I HAD announced my transition, the question most asked by friends and acquaintances was how all the others had reacted. To which I could only reply that they had mainly asked how all the others had reacted.

Apparently people don't yet know what to think of the phenomenon of changing one's sex, and so they ask for help in forming their opinion. In an effort to solve this dilemma, I have decided to tell them how considerate everyone else is and how most transsexuals live their lives with relatively few problems. This gives the collective reaction a positive momentum. But it would be irresponsible of me to deny that there is also a certain degree of opposition from within society.

The importance of being invisible

Paul Gallico's novella *Love of Seven Dolls* (1954) starts with a rather nonchalant sentence. 'In Paris, in the spring of our times, a young girl was about to throw herself into the Seine.' I have always liked the light tone of this first passage, and I can say that for most of my life I, too, have been about to throw myself into the Seine. Although interviewers apparently like to hear me expound all the issues I have been 'grappling with' at length, I don't have much more to say than that. Gallico's nonchalance perfectly expresses the way I feel.

But I should not impose my preference for a lighter tone on other people. And I should not imply that the ease with which I have now proved to be able to cross the borders between the sexes is enjoyed by everyone. I am a 'Sunday's child', as people never tire of telling me – I was born lucky and everything I touch turns to gold – but that cannot be said of everyone who is planning to transform. It actually cannot even be said of me.

Without being overly dramatic, the truth is that there is still a lot of social resistance to overcome. Almost 80 countries still consider homosexuality and various forms of trans identification a crime, mostly without making much of a distinction between them all. Even when the law is on the side of transgender people, society can make life very difficult for them. Social resistance can lead to abuse or even murder – 200 take place a year worldwide – but also to more mundane forms of misfortune, such as being sacked from your job or rejected by your family, church or neighbourhood. From the stories I hear, I know that coming out in southern Texas or Ohio is not easy. And in countries that are otherwise pretty tolerant, like the Netherlands, the reactions can sometimes be intimidating and distressing.

Many classic transsexuals solve these problems by hiding themselves away from the limelight. This is known as 'going stealth'. The lucky ones are soon no longer recognizable as having undergone a transition and therefore no longer find themselves having to discuss the matter with everyone they happen to come across.

Although stealth provides good protection from unwanted attention and discrimination, it can also generate a perpetual fear of being discovered, exposed or betrayed. Hence my urgent appeal to the friends and acquaintances of someone who has undergone a transition not to talk about it to others – not even in countries like the Netherlands. It must be possible, for whatever reason, to become invisible again.

Brave

For me, being invisible in the workplace is out of the question. I don't have the kind of job I can give up and move to the other side of the country to start all over again under a new name. The female estate agent who sent me an email to let me know how much she disapproved of me making my decision public – 'a bit "provocative" if you ask me' – overestimated my talent for changing my sex role in secret. The many people who have told me how 'brave' they think I am for going public also forget that secrecy was not an option.

Don't get me wrong, I appreciate the kindness of these reactions enormously, but if you think about it a little longer, you will see that compliments about my bravery are in fact signs of disapproval. Whether you call it brave or provocative, you are proclaiming that a sex change is so scandalous and shocking that no one else would even dream of mentioning it. Only someone as provocative, no, as brave as I am would put such an offensive announcement in the newspaper.

Violence

And so to the real problems. Through its Trans Murder Monitoring (TMM) Project, Transgender Europe (TGEU) monitors violent crimes against transgender people. In its most recent report, 1,123 murders were reported in 57 countries worldwide between the beginning of 2008 and the end of 2012. The study showed that the numbers are increasing. During the same period, 71 murders were recognized in Europe as being trans-related. Yet, according to Amnesty, very few European countries – only Sweden, Scotland and Croatia – recognize gender identity as a possible motive for murder in their penal codes. That, they claim, is why motives for murder are not examined thoroughly. Of course, you can question whether it is necessary to distinguish different motives for murder in the penal code, but monitoring gender identity as a motive for murder does not seem like a bad idea in itself.

According to a recent report by the Netherlands Institute for Social Research, thirteen trans-related incidents were registered by the police in the Netherlands in 2010. Research by the Institute itself showed that in the past year 5 per cent of the transgender people asked had been threatened in public spaces, 5 per cent had been sexually intimidated, 2 per cent had had property destroyed and 2 per cent had been attacked physically. Forty per cent of the respondents, however, stated that they had never had a single negative response – not even disapproving looks or feeble jokes.

Unemployment

When the British public voted Luke Anderson the winner of the television programme *Big Brother* in 2012, he was the second transsexual candidate to win this popularity contest, after Nadia Almada won in 2004. What more could you wish for from the viewpoint of emancipation?

Nevertheless, after his victory, Anderson's reaction was telling. 'I don't think it has sunk in yet. A big part of it was about acceptance. My whole life I have been an outsider. Thank you so much.' In other words, transgenders often do quite well in society, but they continue to be surprised by that fact.

A publication by the Netherlands Institute for Social Research, *Be Who You Are* (December 2012), shows that transgender people experience more social and mental problems than average. This applies not only to transsexuals who undergo treatment, but to the large group of people who are unhappy with their gender identity. Nearly 40 per cent of them do not have a job and a relatively large group of 17 per cent are unfit for work. Various earlier studies produced the same results. Transgenders are well educated compared with the rest of the population, but their incomes are relatively low.

As far as I can tell, none of these studies have yet discovered what causes transgender people to lag behind. Is it harder for them to find a job? Or do their personal circumstances and mental state make it more difficult to work? Many of those who took part in the survey said they suffered from depression and had suicidal tendencies. On the basis of my own experience, I suspect that it is hard for them to distinguish to what extent their depressed state of mind is caused by their own difficult condition and to what extent by their fear of other people's reactions. What's more, it is difficult to determine how far those fears are justified.

It is a fact that suicide occurs relatively frequently among transgender people, and suicidal thoughts even more often.

Lack of care

In the Netherlands criticism from wider society aimed at the treatment of gender dysphoria mainly focuses on money; at least in my own case, the rare unpleasant reactions that reached me mostly centred on the costs of the medical treatment.

As always, the Internet was a treasury of kindness. One reader on the website of a serious newspaper responded with feeling: 'Let this nearly-50-year-old mess around with her gender. As long as I don't have to pay for it and above all don't have to put up with his pieces in the paper any longer.' One or two people vented their anger towards me personally by email. I can reassure Mrs H., who hoped that I paid for the transition myself and that I would not sell any more books because of it, that I will eventually come out of the process worse off financially.

Society's unwillingness to pay for the medical care of people who are on the brink of despair is remarkable. Acceptance seems to be widespread, but behind the bickering over the costs lies a lack of information, empathy and consequently acceptance, which manifests itself in a lack of care.

Today horrendously long waiting lists mean that you have to wait eighteen months for a first diagnostic consultation at the specialized gender clinic of the vu University Medical Center in Amsterdam. It can then easily take another nine months for the medical treatment to start. For politicians, the care of transsexuals is clearly a low priority. And young doctors tend to prefer other specializations, so the lack of care is partly due to a lack of trained doctors. At the same time the costs are driven up by the strict requirements with which the transition has to comply. To have your sex officially changed so that you can travel with a passport stating your correct sex, you need to undergo more radical medical treatment than many people would themselves want. As mentioned earlier, in some European countries, for instance, you can only get your sex changed in official records if you have been sterilized, a requirement that is completely unnecessary from a transsexual's point of view. Apart from being a violation of human dignity, this needless medical treatment is also dangerous and expensive.

Another problem is that for access to paid care, you need a diagnosis. You have to make it clear that you suffer from a 'gender identity disorder'. In other words, you must prove that you are mentally ill in order to get medical treatment; at the same time you have to prove that you are mentally competent enough to cope with the transition, but not so mentally competent that you can muddle on as you are for another few years. As the American activist Aydin Kennedy said in an interview: 'It's like you're this kid with a bowl going around begging people to put soup in it.'

Let me word this cautiously. To avoid both the costs of care and the frustrations of those seeking it from rising any further, it wouldn't do any harm to adjust the medical procedures a little here and there.

Happy

A few months into my transition, people would ask me 'Are you happy now?' Some pre-empted the answer and said: 'Now you're happy. Now you are who you always have been.'

Although this sounded as though they were putting words in my mouth, as well as being rather dismissive of the social tensions of such a transition, I think you do indeed become happy when you start living according to the image you have of yourself. So, yes, I'm sure that I will soon be perfectly happy.

six

Testosterone

'WHAT IS TESTOSTERONE actually made from?' my
girlfriend asks me, practical as always. And, in an
obvious attempt to encourage me: 'Natural sources?
Do they have to abuse animals to get it?'

Not an unimportant question, considering that
I don't produce testosterone myself and will have to take
it for the rest of my life. I should indeed find out more
about its origins and background. Unfortunately I have
little affinity with medical science or pharmaceutical
matters; to be honest, I know nothing about them at all.
And so, in the first few months of taking the hormones,
I went searching for information, because we won't have
anything to do with animal abuse in our house.

The first thing I came across was the blog of a
transman called Gender Outlaw, probably because
I had searched for the terms 'testosterone' and 'animals'.
Gender Outlaw had consulted a traditional Chinese
medicine doctor who had given him pills containing
testosterone extracted from ostrich penis. Since Gender
Outlaw apparently reads Chinese fluently, he had been

able to trace the origin of the testosterone pills back to the website of a company in Singapore, where they are called Jin Tuo Yang. The pills, which cost around €20 each, were bright blue. Gender Outlaw wrote in a matter-of-fact manner: 'In China, it's believed that consuming animal penis enhances sexual vitality. Penises of yak, water buffalo, deer, antelope, goat, bull, and snake are all served up at specialty penis and testicle restaurants.'

For those who did not believe him, he had added some links. One was a link to a BBC News report about the Guolizhuang restaurant in Beijing, a speciality penis emporium where wealthy businessmen and government bureaucrats secure contracts over steaming penis fondues. There was also a link to a short film in which the journalist Adam Yamaguchi bravely tries various flavours and remarks philosophically, 'It looks quite breakfast-sausagey.'

I decided that this kind of testosterone was not for me and went back to the more common sources. So what is testosterone made from? Trying to establish the origins of the hormone I have lying in my drawer, I soon began to suspect that it is synthetic. It is no longer extracted from bulls' testicles but fabricated in laboratories. And, if the chemists' descriptions are anything to go by, it's pretty unpleasant stuff. You need to wear protective glasses and a gas mask when preparing it.

Nanomoles per litre

As I mentioned before, hormone therapy is not temporary. The treatment never comes to an end. After the first two years the major changes in your body will have occurred; after five years, apart from normal ageing, not much else happens. But you must still continue to use testosterone: if you don't, although your voice and beard will remain masculine, your muscle power will decrease and your shape will become more feminine. Not to mention the emotional changes.

There are many different ways to take the hormones, pills being the least popular. Most people opt for injections – weekly, fortnightly or once every three months – or for a gel that you apply to your body daily. After some time the testosterone in your blood reaches a male level, and then it is up to you to keep that level constant. Women naturally produce testosterone as well, but at much lower levels: their values are somewhere around 1 nanomole per litre, while for men the levels vary from 10 to 35 nanomoles per litre (or from 10 to 45; the information is hard to find and varies widely).

Taking testosterone is a tricky business. You can't simply take twice as much to make your voice twice as low. If you use too much, your body converts the surplus into oestrogen, achieving the exact opposite to what you wanted. It can therefore take a while to find the right dosage, especially since everyone responds to the hormone in a different way. I myself started to feel a little depressed after six months. When I had my blood tested, it showed that my testosterone level had dropped to the lower male range. As soon as I increased the dosage, I felt more cheerful again.

It is important to take regular blood tests to make sure that you are not suffering from any nasty side effects. Since I'm no expert, I can't give medical advice, but I can safely say that you should at least keep an eye on your blood pressure, cholesterol and red blood corpuscles, and on your prostate.

Does testosterone make you nicer and more honest?

There are millions of statistics and claims circulating about testosterone. Among motorcyclists and body-builders, for instance, there is a story going around that male criminal lawyers on average have 30 per cent more testosterone in their blood than male public prosecutors. This is a typical example of the kind of information you don't know what to do with, as long as nobody can tell you how testosterone affects your behaviour.

There are many myths about loss of control and increased aggression caused by using synthetic tes-tosterone and the anabolic steroids derived from it. Since the beginning of the financial and banking crises in 2008, the reputation of the male hormone has become even worse than it already was. There were serious proposals to make male bankers take female hormones, and Jóhanna Sigurðardóttir, former prime minister of Iceland and famous for being the world's first openly lesbian head of government, vowed in her electoral campaign to end the 'age of testosterone'. She said that male leadership had led the country to the verge of bankruptcy and now it was time for oestrogen to take over.

There is indeed a lot of scientific research showing that male bankers and stock traders are driven to recklessness by their testosterone. English neuroscientist John Coates of Cambridge University, formerly a Wall Street trader himself, says that your testosterone level rises when you take risks and are successful. When the level rises past a certain point, however, the risks become irresponsibly large and the successes decrease rapidly. According to Coates, the markets would be more stable if more women and older men were to trade at a high level.

It is reports like these, and stories of bodybuilders who lose control when they've taken too much testosterone, that often cause transmen to start their hormone treatment with trepidation. They – or their partners – are afraid of becoming more aggressive and wilder and they watch themselves anxiously. In almost all cases, however, these fears prove unfounded. As long as the amount of testosterone in the blood does not rise above the normal values and the level remains stable, a transman will not suddenly turn into a caveman and start looting and pillaging. I have no desire to race through traffic-free areas on a scooter, sounding my horn loudly; testosterone makes me no less careful nor more competitive than I already was, nor more irrational. All in all, it would be interesting to consult transsexual men too when researching the effects of testosterone. I suspect that the hypotheses could be adjusted here and there.

In any case, science itself is already debunking the myth of testosterone as the source of all evil. A much quoted Swiss study by neuroscientist Christoph Eisenegger and his colleagues – published in *Nature* journal in 2010 under the title 'Prejudice and Truth about the Effect of Testosterone on Human Bargaining Behaviour' – showed that testosterone made people fairer and more sociable in their behaviour. The researchers did not look at high testosterone values, but at the effect of taking testosterone itself. Female subjects were asked to divide an amount of money among themselves and others. Women who had been administered testosterone divided the money more fairly than women in the control group. What's more, they disagreed less on how to do it.

The study also produced another interesting finding: the women who knew in advance that they were to be given testosterone actually behaved more aggressively and less fairly. The hormone's bad reputation proved to have a greater influence on their behaviour than its positive effect.

A recent study by Matthias Wibral and his colleagues at the Center for Economics and Neuro-science (CENS) at Bonn University showed that male subjects with high testosterone levels have relatively little tendency to lie – probably out of pride and fear of losing face. I have not yet been able to find how this relates to the tendency of criminal lawyers and public prosecutors to lie.

Tough

'Drop by sometime,' says my friend the writer, 'and I'll show you how my chainsaw works.' I have just told him that I have started hormone therapy and this is his way of saying something kind about it. When I tell this story to my granddaughters, who are eight and ten years old at the time, they first start to grin, then giggle and then shake with laughter. They don't make any noise, but they bounce up and down in their chairs with delight. They are laughing at him, I realize, and perhaps they are laughing at me, too.

Six months later, I'm standing looking at my car on a road out in the country. It's stuck in the mud and I'm wondering what to do. Then men appear from all directions, with tow ropes and screwdrivers to prise loose the flap behind which the towing ring is apparently fixed – and for the first time in my life I realize with horror that maybe I should do something, too. Perhaps people expect me to take action now I'm full of testosterone. Should I take a course? By that time, I've been through six months of conversations in which everyone has had a ball making cheap jokes about my masculinity. 'Will you finally now be better at sports?' friend M. asks wittily. As if masculinity and sport are synonymous. 'No,' I say, 'I'll be just as useless as before.'

In the second half of my life, I'll have exactly the same shortcomings as I had in the first half. Testosterone won't change that. At the most, I have become a little more direct in how I react: I'm more likely to give as good as I get, and get over my irritation more quickly. But the hormone will not make me much tougher. I have heard from other transmen that they no longer cry – but I never did that to begin with.

seven

Relationships

I WAS A LESBIAN for one afternoon of my life. When I was thirteen, after wondering for my whole life what was wrong with me, I met a girl in the orthodontist's waiting room who gave me the pleasant illusion that I was a lesbian. For the rest of the afternoon I walked around triumphantly with that thought in my mind, happy that I could finally explain myself to myself. Then, in the evening, I realized that though I was getting close, this still did not explain everything. Something else was wrong, too.

In the years that followed, the word kept coming up nonetheless when I told people that my romantic feelings focused on women.

'Oh, you're a lesbian!'
'No,' I would say, 'I'm not a lesbian, I'm a homosexual.'
'So what's the difference?'
'Being a lesbian is for women.'

Nobody understood, of course. I didn't even understand it myself completely, which was precisely my intention. Later still, I reconciled myself to the accursed label for practical reasons. Being a lesbian never came easily to me, but that's what I was, until I wasn't any more.

Harry Benjamin, transsexuality and homosexuality

In November 1966 the *New York Times* published an article on transsexuality. Johns Hopkins Hospital, one of the most renowned academic hospitals in the United States, had established a gender clinic and started to treat people. Until then surgery had mainly been performed in Europe, Morocco, Japan and Mexico, but now America was about to catch up.

The article quoted doctors who, after much thought, had become convinced of the seriousness of the situation and that requests for medical help were genuine. One psychiatrist-psychoanalyst from Los Angeles had found, to his surprise, nothing strange about the transsexuals he had examined. 'They are shockingly normal', he exclaimed. Apart from that one thing, then.

The key figure in these developments in America was the endocrinologist Dr Harry Benjamin of the Harry Benjamin Foundation. According to the *New York Times*, Benjamin originally coined the term 'transsexual' in 1966. In the same year he had published the influential book *The Transsexual Phenomenon*, which had helped to clarify the terminology. He described transsexuality as an independent phenomenon rather than a symptom of mental illness.

In retrospect Harry Benjamin was clearly one of the first to emphasize the difference between gender identity and sexual preference. Transsexuality is about who you are, while homosexuality and heterosexuality are about your preference for a partner. Yet Benjamin did not publicly conclude that transsexuals can just as well be homosexual as heterosexual. In his book all the transsexual women are attracted to men and all the transsexual men to women. In reality, however, both groups are so 'shockingly normal' that in this sense too they are just like everyone else: most transmen prefer a woman as partner, but there are also homosexual transmen. And lesbian transwomen. And bisexual transgenders of all kinds.

Love

When it comes to romantic and sexual attraction between people, there is little you can say with any certainty. All's fair in love and war – even a sex change, and I find it strange that commentators are so eager to label, classify, categorize, standardize and, above all, understand the romantic relationships of those who undergo transition. There is nothing to be understood. Love in general is beyond our understanding. Why do people stay together when one of them decides to live the rest of his life as a man? The answer I came across most, even in intellectual considerations of this sticky question, is that perhaps his female partner suddenly became heterosexual. But of course the lesbian partner has not suddenly turned heterosexual: she is still a lesbian. It's just that her partner is now a man. But should she dump him for such a trifling matter?

Reports regularly present alarming figures on the relationship status of people who have changed their sex role. If they don't have a partner already, it often turns out to be difficult to find one. If they do have a partner, the change can lead to divorce; the number of divorces resulting from one partner undergoing a transition is many times higher than for the rest of the population. But I get a much less dismal impression from stories I have heard myself. Existing relationships often seem to survive, while singles are remarkably successful at entering into new ones.

My own impressions may be different from those propagated in the media because I mainly know of men who used to live as lesbians prior to their change. It is generally believed within the transsexual community that the relationships of these men are much more likely to last than those of women who used to live as men in a heterosexual relationship. This difference is probably due to the fact that partners in homosexual relationships have already talked at length about the meaning of femininity and masculinity; they have had to figure out and unravel both their own identity and their partner's. That makes the blow of the transition less severe than in a heterosexual marriage.

But even these classic marriages can survive the storm of the transition.

Of course, you have no right to expect your partner to stay with you after all the changes you have gone through, just as you never, in any relationship, have a right to assume that your partner wants to stay with you. All in all, the only sensible thing to be said about it is that, statistics or not, you can never predict what will happen in any given situation. In this respect, too, the situation is shockingly normal.

Grief

The consternation you cause by undergoing the transition! I received many letters from people who talked about an intangible feeling of loss, which they described as 'grief': the loss of my female persona, which they had known and cherished for so long and which, in their eyes, would now be gone forever. One would have liked some kind of 'farewell service' with coffee and cake; another dreamed of lying on a settee with me, clasping me in a melancholic embrace; others wrote obituaries full of RIPs and expressed their 'deep sadness' at my passing. It was all a little macabre, especially as I am of course still here.

Grief is a well-known response to transition, although some experience it more intensely than others. Personally I think that feelings of grief mostly affect your parents and siblings, who lose their grip on the shared past that seems so intimately linked to your name. Ultimately they will have to realize that there are no hermetically sealed barriers between your past and your present: that you are still part of that shared past and that nothing has really been lost.

Partners become aware of this more quickly as, all being well, they know who you are and therefore that you have not disappeared. I recently heard a young transman ask his girlfriend ironically if she had properly grieved during his transition. 'Did you mourn me? Did I die?' She burst out laughing and said no, of course not. Which was understandable since, after all, he was sitting right there next to her.

Yet partners do lose something. During the transition, it is they who have to do most of the work. They have to get used to your physical changes, your change of name and how they should address you, your social role, the shift in your relationship. They have to deal with your temporary egocentrism and in many cases readjust their vision of the future.

On the Internet, I have followed the stories of two beautiful and kind young people, both originally from a small rural community in the southern states of America. Many years ago, separately, they liberated themselves from the pressure of their surroundings. They ended their relationships with men and proudly announced that they were lesbians. In this emancipated state, the two young women met, married at a wonderful wedding ceremony that was not recognized by law, and would have lived happily ever after if one of them had not shortly afterwards decided to live from then on as a man.

For the partner, this meant not only a radical change in the relationship, but a social upheaval. Suddenly rebellion and liberation no longer seemed relevant; she was right back to square one. She had just managed to persuade the rather unsympathetic accountant at her work that her relationship had the status of a marriage, and now she had to go and tell him that she was married legally after all, as the relationship was now heterosexual. Fortunately this fairy tale had a happy ending: the couple now have a child and are just as happy as any other model American family.

Of course, partners are not the only ones who have to actively readjust their relationship with a transsexual. Children seem to lose their grip even more so, if this is possible, when their father or mother has a sex change. Sometimes things go wrong and the relationship is damaged; in other cases it goes really well. The key to success could very well be that children should not get the feeling that they are going to lose the mother or father they had. The son who addressed his mother as 'Mr my mother' seems to have found a brilliant solution.

Finally, when you go through the transition, you yourself lose part of your past: it is harder, for instance, to reminisce in the company of strangers. But despite all these trials and tribulations, there is good news: you are still who you are. There is no need for condolences.

eight

Woman: 'If I Were a Man . . .'

EVERY WOMAN CARRIES an invisible man around with her. It still frequently happens that as a woman you don't get served in a restaurant or in the breakfast room of a hotel before that invisible man has arrived. When you travel together as two women, receptionists say, 'Ah, ladies, out and about on your own?' When you attend a club meeting, people ask you during the drinks afterwards, 'And what brings you here? Is your husband on the committee?' When you buy a car, the salesman says, 'What will your boyfriend say?'

In Italy I once entered a bar with my girlfriend.

'Oh, so sad', the barman said. 'All alone! Where are your husbands?'
'We killed them', we sighed.
'Ha ha', laughed the barman, shocked.

Opinions on men

Why do women so often say that they would rather be a man? Not, I suspect, because they hold men in higher esteem than women. Now that I'm a man, I'm a little shocked at the opinions I hear from women in the constant conversations I have about masculinity and femininity. Men, they say, are bastards. Men consider you a secondary species. Men are dangerous, not to be trusted. They are egocentric and only interested in other men.

During the first six months of my transition, women would still apologize when they expressed such opinions. 'We don't mean you', they would grin. But after six months, when my voice had dropped and my body looked more masculine, they became more distrustful.

'I don't know if I can keep on telling you every-thing', some women said. 'I still start my emails with "dear",' others wrote, 'but actually I never do that with men. You always have to be so careful.' At first, such remarks sounded quite light-hearted, but as time passed they became more serious.

It indeed remains to be seen whether I'm still to be trusted. I believe so, but perhaps I am already unconsciously writing about women from a corrupt, male perspective. So just to be on the safe side, let me discuss a theme that I became interested in a long time ago, when I was still running on oestrogen. In films, stories and songs I heard women describe what they would do if they were a man, a good preparation for my future life.

Here, too, it was mainly prejudices against men that came up. First, the women said that, as soon as they were a man, they would finally be able to function normally without the invisible man permanently at their side. Second, since men do it all the time, they would lie and cheat with a vengeance. And third, women would of course be far better men.

Women are better men than men

Because of my interest in sex changes, I once watched the documentary *Dream Girls* (1994) – about the Japanese Takarazuka Revue actresses – with great fascination. The theatre company was founded in 1914 to promote the Takarazuka railway line and always had an all-woman cast. The male parts were therefore also played by women, in itself not very unusual. What was remarkable about the transvestite roles of the Takarazuka actresses was the way they affected the females in the audience, many of whom became infatuated with the women performing as men.

Men, the fans said with revulsion on their faces, are brutes. But the Takarazuka men were different: they were subtle, tender and attentive. Give us a man like that, the Japanese women sighed at the doors of the theatre. Give us a girl from the Takarazuka Revue!

After *Dream Girls*, I watched the documentary *Shinjuku Boys* (1995), about three Japanese women who worked as male escorts in a nightclub in Tokyo. Like the Takarazuka actresses, the escorts were also seen as ideal men by their female admirers. When one of them, a transsexual called Tatsu, started hormone therapy, customers complained that he was becoming a typical man, saying: 'Now you're not nice anymore.'

Both films portrayed mainly heterosexual women looking for a type of man that they could not find in their daily life, and whom they longed for desperately: elegant, attentive and respectful. I have to say that as a Dutch viewer, I was rather surprised at the deep contempt and aversion with which these ordinary Japanese women talked about their ordinary Japanese cis men at home.

The cheerful way in which Dutch women complain about Dutch men was nothing compared to the vehemence of these grievances. It made me think at the time that the emancipation of women has done men's reputation a lot of good. Once relations between the sexes are more balanced, satisfaction is greater on both sides. Feminism, often seen in the West as hatred of men, is in fact very well-favoured towards men. It enhances not only the interests of women, but of men and society as a whole – as only becomes clear when you focus on the disdain women feel for men in countries where tasks and opportunities are not fairly shared.

If I were a man, I'd do something about it

In the film *Victor/Victoria* (1982) – in which Julie Andrews plays a woman who pretends to be a man who pretends to be a woman – the singer Victoria says that there have been times in her life when she wished she were a man.

> 'Why, for heaven's sake?' asks her manager, Toddy.
> 'Oh, that's easy', says Victoria. 'If I were a man, I could do a lot of things a woman never can.'
> 'Like what, for example?' asks Toddy.
> 'Be free to plot and plan, free to live my life without permission from a man. What a lovely life I'd plan, if I were a man.'

She would build all the tallest buildings, explore every far off land and learn how to fly: 'Doing all that fellas do, but better!'

The film is set in the year 1934. That makes sense, you think: a woman in that era would still long for male privileges and duties. In the First World War, for instance, the American army recruited soldiers with a poster featuring the young Bernice Smith wearing a uniform and the text 'Gee!! I wish I were a man, I'd join the Navy.'

Smith really said these words, in all innocence, and her genuine admiration for male responsibilities can be heard in them. The same attitude could also be found in female characters in novels and comic books of the first half of the twentieth century. In 1941, in the famous *Green Lantern* comic books, the young Irene Miller found herself confronted with an imminent epidemic. 'No serum . . . people dying of pneumonia . . .', she wailed. 'Oh – if I were a man – I'd do something about this!'

In our own time, we can no longer really understand such regret on the part of females. Nowadays everyone can fight and save mankind, so why would you want to be a man? And yet the desire has by no means disappeared, as you can see if you take popular culture seriously. Without actively searching, over the years I have come across quite a lot of texts in which women dream of all the fantastic things they could do with their lives . . . if only they were a man! Stop whining, you find yourself mumbling as an emancipated onlooker, get up and do something, go and study mechanical engineering, whatever. But the women know for certain that such a foolhardy venture is impossible.

My all-time favourite in this genre is still the rather bizarre song '*Si j'étais un homme*' by Diane Tell, in which she not only imagines herself becoming a captain on an elegant green-and-white boat, but also passionately declares her love to a woman. At least, she sings, 'if I were a man, but I am a woman, and a woman doesn't do things like that'.

We could consider it a needlessly complicated lesbian song, were it not that the singer can only imagine buying flowers and jewellery for her loved one and having a villa built in Bergamo if she were a man. The song is certainly not meant to have lesbian connotations, or to be a play on gender identities. On the contrary it is a rather naive complaint about the lack of romance in modern heterosexual relationships; but apparently it is up to men to change that. 'I am a woman and, as a woman, you don't do such things.'

At the end of 2010, an editor of the popular website AfterEllen also noticed the number of female singers expressing the wish to be a man. A couple of years earlier, Beyoncé sang 'If I Were a Boy', the Pussycat Dolls 'If I Was a Man', Ciara 'Like a Boy', Fefe Dobson 'If I Was a Guy' and Jessie J 'Do It Like a Dude'. This was no longer a theme: it was a trend.

The songs were not so much about the noble desire to become the captain of a ship. They mainly revolved around 'doing' and cheating on as many girls as possible. 'If I was a guy . . . I would be so horny, yeah, yeah', 'I would grab my crotch', 'lie', 'fool your heart', 'I would do loads of chicks', 'with force'. 'I would turn off my phone, tell everyone it's broken, so they'd think that I was sleeping alone.' 'I'd be a cowboy, I'd terrify you with my gun.'

Clearly this trend is based on a rather uncomplicated notion of maleness – yeah, yeah.

The subtleties of the ordinary man

When all is said and done, I don't believe I've learned much about manliness from all these films and songs. At the most, I've learned something about women. Women in popular culture do not find it easy to break loose from the invisible man who hangs over them like a dominant shadow. That explains the persistent desire to *be* a man, which offers a woman two possible solutions for the problem of male awfulness. You become a better man, or you don't become a better man but you don't care, because now you are a man, so you can be a bastard and an egotist.

If I may hazard a guess, I would say that these solutions mainly feature in fantasies. It is in the imagination that stereotypes thrive. When women have been humiliated by men, they picture their revenge in sharp and extreme contrasts. But as soon as it becomes serious, and women really move in the direction of masculinity, the nuances return. At least I hope that, as a new man, I have neither the obligation to be endlessly understanding nor the arduous task of conquering all women, one by one. Just being an ordinary man seems difficult enough to me.

nine

Man: 'As if Men Have it So Easy!'

'IT'S A GOOD THING', says one of my friends as he greets me with a kiss, 'that I'm a man-kissing man. Otherwise we'd have to stop doing this.'

Others are less open in expressing it, but here and there I notice a little hesitation when it comes to kissing. Some of my male friends have stopped finishing off their emails with 'love', using 'kind regards' instead, and start them with 'hi' rather than 'dear'. There is no doubt about it: I've entered a new world. Kissing and touching are fortunately something of the past and, to my great relief, public displays of affection are no longer expected of me.

In the first year of my life as a man I was not sure what to do when I saw a baby. Smile? Not smile? At first I was afraid that I would reveal my past history if I were too enthusiastic in the presence of babies, but then I decided that my natural sangfroid makes me look manly enough – I don't have to change anything in that respect. So I smile reservedly at babies; I don't kiss them, but I do say 'hi' very affectionately.

Fate

Men don't have it easy. That much has become clear to me since I announced my switch to the male domain. People have been writing to me to point out the disadvantages of my decision. I might think that I am now in a privileged position, they say, but in reality men have drawn the short straw.

The complaint I hear most from men is about shaving: women get out of bed and they're ready to go. They don't have to do anything else about their appearance, but men . . .! Shaving seems to be a heavy burden for every man, and my objection that women, too, take great pains over their looks each morning is invariably brushed aside. The second frequently expressed complaint is more serious and concerns the responsibility men feel about their male task, and how little recognition they get for fulfilling it. It's a man's world; but are women grateful for that? No way!

When Barack Obama beat Mitt Romney in the u.s. elections, the German newspaper *Die Zeit* wrote that minorities had now finally come together to become the majority, and that they will probably continue to do so. American white men – descendants of the pilgrims who founded the United States – are at the beginning of this century outnumbered by a coalition of women, diverse ethnic groups and members of the LGBT community.

In Europe the demographic numbers are different, for the time being at least. Here ethnic groups are not yet that large. White men mainly have to deal with an increasingly powerful majority of women. The newspaper wondered how Western men can best withdraw from the world's centre stage. How should they respond to losing their power and status? And especially while women are still making their demands and want men to be both sensitive and virile at the same time.

You can conclude from this that contemporary man finds himself in dire straits. As always, he continues to be blamed for his dominant position, while knowing that he will not be able to retain it. From the occasional letter in my mailbox, I gather that the writer has not had much luck in complaining about this onerous fate. 'Now you're a man,' he says, 'you'll have to get used to no longer getting away with playing the role of victim. That's the exclusive preserve of women.'

The shocked transman

Don't think I'm trying to say that men have an easy time of it. You can object and say that men still enjoy enough respect in the world, that their position is still inviolable. But in the last year I have heard too many stories from transmen who have been shocked by the disdain with which women treat men as a matter of course.

For the transsexual man it can come as a shock to discover that he can no longer take on the role of victim; the assumed dominance of men suddenly makes him, too, an acceptable target of aggression and ridicule.

I once heard a twenty-year-old transman describe in bewilderment how a young woman in a bar had hit him pretty hard just because he was standing in her way. What seemed to upset him most was that bystanders had no sympathy for him at all when he protested.

It is because of the persistent prejudices surrounding men that some women treat them with little respect. A young father who went to town to do groceries a couple of days after his child had been born was loudly accused of being egocentric by a woman in a shop. How could he cheerfully walk around town while his wife was still in bed recovering from childbirth? Describing the encounter in a film on YouTube, the transman was clearly upset, saying:

> I was so baffled, I didn't say anything to her. But that same attitude, assuming that the father is just going to be selfish and worthless in this situation, has surfaced a few times already. It has really bothered me, you know. Personality and character-wise, I'm caring and I can be very selfless in situations like this. I have no problem taking up all the slack while my wife is healing. I don't have to be told to take up the slack – I want to. And yet I've got all these people imposing these negative male stereotypes on me and it's really irritating me. And not just as a transman, but as a man!

These men are shocked because until recently they had lived as women and were not used to this kind of treatment. In her book about her time undercover as a man,

Norah Vincent criticizes the condescension with which men are rejected when they try to make contact with women in a bar or a club. What is understandable from a woman's point of view – defensive behaviour to keep horny men at bay – proves to be humiliating from the male perspective and harmful to men's self-respect. Men are not only humiliated on the world stage, but in their personal lives.

Transmen would make good diplomats, travelling between the male and female domains with inside information to explain the different standpoints. At the very least, they could clarify men's terrible pushiness, which women resist so vehemently. If anyone understands the powerful effects of testosterone, it's them. 'I'm sorry', transmen say in their confessions on YouTube. 'I'm sorry that I used to call men pigs. Now I understand that they can't do anything about it.'

Privileged position

Okay, okay, okay, I can hear you say, but what men have to fear most is other men. Compared to that, the treatment they receive from women is nothing. And you would be right.

I can't say much yet about power relations elsewhere, but in the street I have already had to get used to the idea that I have suddenly become visible to men again. As a woman I had become invisible in recent years, but now young men in the big city all of a sudden look at me provocatively, brush past me and are clearly aware of my presence. I don't think I look particularly aggressive, but they probably see the undeniable arrogance of my appearance as a challenge. Either way, they are sizing me up. When transmen note with surprise how dangerous the streets have become, they are mainly referring to the physical threat posed by other men.

All in all, you can sympathize with men. They are losing political power, they are losing ground in the workplace, they can't always count on the sympathy of women and they stand in each other's way. And yet there are still no long lists of songs by men saying they would rather be a woman, like those by women dreaming of being a man. I don't feel that I've lost many privileges because of my social migration – on the contrary. Men still have the privileged social position that they have enjoyed for a long time.

I can well understand a couple of ardently ideological women recently accusing me of having deserted to the enemy – if you can't beat them, join them – and of having betrayed women. Fortunately none of them were very serious but, for me too, it's a strange idea that I'm suddenly functioning as the white heterosexual man I have always regarded with some suspicion. As a kind of rebound response, I have the feeling that since I 'defected' I have become more of a feminist than ever before.

Mr X

In the course of my life, I have served on many evaluation committees and juries. At the meetings of these groups there is always a hope that the person selected at the end of the process will be a woman.

So many women are put forward, discussed, considered, but alas, they all lack something . . . talent? No, they have talent, the members of the committee say. Respect! Yes, this woman has a lot of merits, few can hold a candle to her. No, it's something else, something like . . . charisma, yes, that's it. An aura of authority! It's a shame, but we'll have to choose Mr X after all. He's got authority. And charisma. Of course we would much prefer a woman, but not one of them has the authority or charisma of Mr X.

Maybe, says one of the wittier committee members, he could have a sex change. Hilarity all round. We'll suggest it to him, the others say. For the position and the money we're offering him, it's the least he can do.

There's little to be done about this. It is a pity, though, that in all my long years of listening to such conversations, not once have I seen the man who was finally appointed actually choosing to live as a woman from then on. Not once!

ten

Famous Figures

YOUR LIFE IS NOT shaken up and turned upside down by conversations you follow from a to z, but by snippets you pick up at random here and there.

At some stage in my youth I was struck by something I heard on the television about Casablanca. I was probably on my way to bed when I caught a few words of a broadcast about the French surgeon Georges Burou, who had been a specialist in the field of sex reassignment surgery in the Clinique du Parc, 13 Rue La Pebie, Casablanca, Morocco, since the 1950s.

Burou was by no means the first doctor to perform such operations, but he had devised a highly modern method of creating female genitals from male ones, which had assured him an exclusive clientele. In 1958, for instance, he had operated on the singer Jacqueline Charlotte Dufresnoy, who performed at the Paris club Le Carrousel under the name Coccinelle. Colleagues of Coccinelle, including Bambi and April Ashley, also visited Dr Burou in Casablanca.

Once the operation had been performed success-fully, you could have your birth certificate modified and enter into matrimony as a woman. In 1960 Coccinelle married at Notre-Dame in Paris with full ceremony, only to file for divorce a couple of years later on the grounds that she was actually a man. April Ashley was married in 1963 and was from then on known as Lady Corbett. Shortly afterwards her marriage was annulled on the same grounds.

These nightclub and film stars bouncing back and forth pragmatically between female and male identities obviously didn't do much to advance the cause of emancipation. After Coccinelle's divorce, the French state stopped modifying official records and Ashley's divorce had the same effect in the UK and Australia.

Back then I didn't know all that. I had only heard 'Casablanca' and 'sex change' and I was sold on the idea. The fact that it only applied to men taking on a female identity was something that either passed me by or was not mentioned in the half-sentence I heard. All I knew was that I had to go to Casablanca if I wanted to follow my destiny in life. Counting back, I think I must have taken this first mental step midway through the 1970s.

After that I did nothing more about it for many years. Although I did search public libraries for infor-mation on transition in my late adolescence, I was not inspired by what I read. It smacked of social work and tended to describe transsexuality as a kind of drab and deprived tumour on the margins of society.

My inner aspirations were only revived when I switched on the television one night and heard the last sentence of a documentary about Queen Christina of Sweden. 'She abdicated,' the narrator said, 'and lived henceforth as a man.' Now that was a life perspective I could imagine for myself. With every step I took in my adult life after that, I imagined that one fine day I would leave this glorious career behind me and adopt a radically different role. 'She abdicated and lived henceforth as a man' became my mantra.

In this chapter I look briefly at the lives of a number of well-known transgender people, mainly to illustrate how people who decide to alter their gender identities start from widely varying situations. Some of the people I portray here did not even tell their later partners that they had changed roles; others openly pioneered new medical treatments and the social opportunities they presented. But no matter what direction their lives took, they were certainly not a drab tumour on the margins of society. They had jobs, gained respect, contributed to science and culture, got married and travelled, sometimes without official documents. And it was not uncommon for them to receive the full cooperation of the authorities, Church and civil servants in all of these endeavours.

Christina of Sweden (1626–1689)
Christina, queen of Sweden, abdicated when she was 27 years old, left Stockholm on a white horse and dressed in

men's clothes, travelled around Europe under the name Count Dohna, converted to Catholicism and, according to some accounts, 'lived henceforth as a man'.

There is much to say about Christina's colourful life. About her efforts to turn Sweden into an enlightened and intellectually progressive country. About her contacts with almost every scientist, sculptor, composer, writer and thinker of her time. About her religious quests, successful peace negotiations, less successful political claims and strategies, and financial debacles.

But I will limit myself here to the question of her alleged masculinity. There are roughly two versions of her life as a man. In the first, Christina was at the very least a lesbian and had a relationship with Ebba Sparre, whom she introduced to the English ambassador as her 'bedfellow'. She threatened to abdicate if the marriage proposals and the persistent pressure to produce an heir to the Swedish throne did not cease. Because of her masculine behaviour and physique, it is often claimed that she was transgender. Perhaps, some say, she was intersexual.

The second version of the story sees these suggestions of homosexuality or transgenderism as nothing but modern projections. Yes, Ebba was Christina's bedfellow, but in the seventeenth century people had bedfellows to keep them warm. If she expressed her passion for women, it should be seen in the light of Renaissance notions of love. There is no proof whatsoever that Christina ever entered into a serious relationship with any of the men and women she favoured. She abdicated purely on religious grounds. And she wore men's shoes because she had been raised as a boy who was later to become king.

Of course, it is impossible to find out what Christina of Sweden herself really felt and thought. It is even impossible to find out what kind of physique she had. Over the centuries the controversy about her masculinity reached such heights that in 1965 her remains were exhumed and examined. That yielded little information, however. It was no longer possible to examine her tissue, as embalmers had removed her organs. And so, fortunately, the mystery of her identity remained largely intact.

We'wha (1849–1896)

We'wha (Way-wah or Weiwa) was a *lhamana*, a synthesis of man and woman. This ambiguous role was part of the culture of the Zuni tribe in New Mexico, to which We'wha belonged. A *lhamana* mixed social roles by wearing both women's and men's clothes, performing male and female tasks, and combining elements of both female and male behaviour within the family. In the Zuni language it was perfectly possible to say 'she is a man' or 'he is a woman'.

We'wha achieved great fame in 1886 when she went to Washington for six months as a Zuni ambassador. She met and talked with President Grover Cleveland, diplomats, lawyers and members of Congress. During these meetings, everyone thought they were dealing with a 'normal' woman.

Much has been written about the life of We'wha. Contemporary anthropologists have speculated whether she would have been welcomed into American high society quite as enthusiastically if it had become known that she was anatomically a man. As a matter of fact, just how enthusiastic the Zuni tribe and other indigenous peoples themselves were about the *lhamana* or Two-spirit People is also a matter of debate.

Karl M. Baer (1885–1956)

When Karl Baer was born, the baby's sex was not immediately clear. 'On superficial inspection,' the physician said, 'the shape makes a feminine appearance. Ergo we are dealing with a girl.' Baer grew up as Martha, studied sociology and pedagogy in Berlin and Hamburg, became a social worker, campaigned against the trafficking of women and as a young adult decided to live henceforth as Karl.

In 2006 the historian Hermann Simon wrote an afterword to the English translation of Baer's autobiography of 1907, in which he relates a story told to him by his great-aunt Margarete. At the beginning of the twentieth century, Margarete was part of a group of young Jewish intellectuals who helped survivors of the Russian pogroms and shared an interest in art and science.

In this circle the aunt became friends with Fräulein Martha Baer, a very intellectual and astute woman who attracted attention through her masculine looks and behaviour. She smoked thick cigars, drank copious amounts of beer and had hair on her face and a distinctly male voice. One day Fräulein Baer unfortunately had to bid farewell to all her friends, as she had found a job elsewhere. But surprise, surprise – a short time later, a young man named Karl Baer joined the group. He was the spitting image of Martha Baer, except his hair was now cut short and he wore men's clothing. Out of pure courtesy and discretion, the friends said nothing and welcomed Karl Baer to the group as their new friend.

In 1906 Baer was diagnosed in hospital with pseudo-hermaphroditism. Through the intervention of Magnus Hirschfeld he received hormone therapy and underwent a number of sex operations. He was one of the first people to undergo such surgery.

Shortly afterwards the sex change was officially recognized. His birth certificate was annotated to confirm his male identity. The text reads: 'The child specified on this certificate is of the male sex and has been given the first name Karl, instead of Martha. Registered by order of the court at Arolsen on 8 January 1907.' On 10 October 1907 Karl married his great love in a synagogue in Vienna.

Baer's half-autobiographical, half-fictional *Aus eines Mannes Mädchenjahren* (*Memoirs of a Man's Maiden Years*) was a huge success. It was translated into several languages and even made into a film in 1919. The book was published under the pseudonym N. O. Body, mainly to indicate that Baer's past life had made him profoundly confused about who he really was – not only as a man with a female past, but also as a German Jew.

In 1920 Baer became director of the Berlin lodges of the Jewish service organization B'nai B'rith. After the forcible closure of the lodges by the Gestapo in 1937, he left for Palestine with his second wife. He later died in Israel. No footage of the film has survived.

Alan L. Hart (1890–1962)

Alan L. Hart was a physician, radiologist and novelist. At the age of eighteen he published the poem 'My Irish Colleen' – a declaration of love to a girl – anonymously in the *Albany College Student* magazine. In 1911 the love poem was reprinted in his college yearbook under his birth name, Lucille Hart.

In his late twenties Hart went into therapy because he was afraid of loud noises. Gradually the conversation turned to his romantic interest in women and his doubts regarding his identity. This led to extensive medical tests, after which his uterus was removed. From then on he began to wear men's clothes.

In 1920 Dr Joshua Gilbert of the University of Oregon, who had treated Hart, published an article in the *Journal of Nervous and Mental Disease* in which he described the case of 'patient H.' at length. About the transformation he wrote, 'Her hair was cut, a complete male outfit was secured . . . she made her exit as a

female and started as a male with a new hold on life and ambitions worthy of her high degree of intellectuality.'
Hart subsequently married his first wife, using the name Robert Allen Bamford Jr.

Hart established himself as a doctor, but his work was initially made difficult by revelations about his past. Later, by then divorced and remarried, he gained a better grip on his career. He studied radiology and became an expert on tuberculosis.

In 1935 he wrote the successful novel *Dr Mallory*, soon followed by *In the Lives of Men*. A critic wrote about the second novel: 'For a doctor, he seems to know surprisingly little of women. His portraits of them are little more than profile sketches. Those he approves are colourless and negative, the others incredibly cold and selfish.'

After their deaths and at the request of Hart and his wife, a fund was established in their names to provide grants in the field of leukaemia research.

Billy Tipton (1914–1989)

For most of his life the jazz musician and bandleader Billy Tipton lived as a man. Only after his death did his wife and children discover that he was anatomically a woman.

Because Tipton had not had sex reassignment therapy, he told the women he lived with that his genitals had been damaged in an accident. His ribs had also been broken so badly that it was necessary to keep binding his chest. You can, of course, ask yourself to what extent these women bought his story; there must have been signs that something else was going on, if only because Tipton was never officially married, although his successive partners were referred to as 'Mrs Tipton' on their driving licences.

Tipton's past history was not revealed until he lay on his deathbed and the chest bindings were removed. His son had witnessed this revelation and, the day after Tipton died, he went to the press with the story, after which it became headline news.

According to a biographer, Billy Tipton showed that 'the "difference" between men and women is largely in the eye of the beholder.' 'Being a man' is not purely a matter of biology, it is a role, a way of behaving and how that behaviour is interpreted by those around you.

Tipton was by no means the only person to successfully play the male role publicly without having had any treatment. A few years after Tipton, gospel singer Wilmer 'Little Ax' M. Broadnax (1916–1994) died, and it was discovered that he, too, had been born as a woman.

Michael Dillon (1915–1962)

At the end of his life Laurence Michael Dillon was ordained as a Tibetan Buddhist monk. He was one of the first Westerners to have this honour conferred upon him.

Dillon was educated at St Anne's College for women at the University of Oxford, but was certain of his male identity and, after graduating, found an interested doctor who was willing to prescribe him hormones.

Before he could take the treatment Dillon had to consult a psychiatrist. Unfortunately the latter decided to bandy the story of the transition all over town. Alarmed, Dillon fled and found a job at a garage in Bristol. He stayed there for four years and worked his way up to become a tow-truck driver. Later he would become a ship's doctor.

Admitted to hospital at some point because of his diabetes, he came into contact with doctors who were willing to perform surgery. Dillon is generally considered to be not only the first person to receive hormone therapy, but the first to undergo a phalloplasty – surgery to construct a penis. It is alleged that Dillon did not enter into relationships with women; apparently he considered that inappropriate since he could not give them children.

In 1944 the authorities changed his name and sex on his birth certificate, much to the dismay of his brother, Sir Robert Dillon, the eighth Baronet of Lismullen, who broke off all contact with him. Fortunately the compilers of *Debrett's Peerage*, which records all details of the British aristocracy, were less faint-hearted. They changed the order of succession in the male line so that Michael would have first claim on the baronetcy on his brother's death.

The victory, however, proved premature. When Sir Robert did indeed die, it emerged that another guide to the aristocracy, *Burke's Peerage*, had not adopted the changes. Consequently one list stated that Sir Robert had a brother and the other that he had a sister. The discrepancy attracted the attention of the *Sunday Express*, which was only too willing to give the matter publicity. Dillon fled again, this time to India, where he went to live in a monastery.

He studied Buddhism, wrote several books, adopted the name Sramanera Jivaka, which he later changed to Lobzang Jivaka, and was ordained as a monk. He died young, exhausted by the hardships of the monastic life. Or of life in general.

Andreas Krieger (1966–)

Heidi Krieger was an East German shotputter who won gold at the 1986 European Championships in Athens. Since having sex reassignment surgery in 1997, Krieger has lived under the name Andreas.

After his career ended, Krieger stated in several trials that his trainers had given him very high doses of anabolic steroids without his knowledge. As a result of the strain on his muscles and joints, he had developed severe physical problems. Furthermore his body and behaviour had become so masculine as a result of taking the hormones that he had become severely confused about his already uncertain sexual identity. In the end Krieger saw no other way out than to undergo a sex change.

He said in interviews that he might have made this decision without the doping, but now the decision had been forced on him without his consent. 'They killed Heidi', he said in an interview with the *New York Times*.

Balian Buschbaum (1980–)

The story of the German athlete Balian Buschbaum brings us up to the modern-day transition. Here there is no forced administration of hormones, no experimental treatments and no concealed physical characteristics. Buschbaum explicitly goes public as a contented man with new attributes.

Before reaching that level of contentment, however, Buschbaum also experienced a long period of emotional uncertainty. 'For many years I had something dark inside of me', he said in a television interview shortly after announcing his transition publicly. He talked about loneliness, despair 'and the infinite rage, which nevertheless helped me escape from being a slave of my own body'.

Buschbaum, national pole-vaulting champion in 1999 and sixth at the Olympic Games in Sydney, decided to end his career as a sportswoman and give full rein to his masculinity. 'I'm doing the whole programme. Removal of breasts. Construction of an artificial penis.'

The fact that Buschbaum has since been rather boastful about the achievements of his penis is not something all transmen thank him for. On discussion forums, they complain that he is drawing undue attention to the differences between men and women and, in doing so, contributing to stereotyping. More philosophical and artistically-minded transmen, who already have to fight against the prejudice that all men are sporty and tough, expect film clips of Buschbaum riding around on a motorcycle to have very little emancipatory impact.

Such complaints are understandable but, in my view, not entirely justifiable. Buschbaum is a sportsman, after all. He likes to recall the erection that lasted 21 hours and 37 minutes when he used his penis pump for the first time and didn't know how to switch it off. And why not? There are countless different types of men, and the macho man is one of them.

Women

Just as people of all kinds of plumage prefer the male role, there are also many who wish to live as a woman. I already mentioned We'wha, who had a combined identity, but went out into the wide world as a woman.

Christine Jorgensen (1926–1989) is the most famous transwoman. She was certainly not the first person to undergo sex reassignment surgery, since these operations had already been performed in the early twentieth century in Germany, but in 1952 the *New York Daily News* claimed that she was. She became world news overnight.

When she returned to America after being treated in Denmark, the press horded around her en masse. Footage of her arrival at Idlewild Airport in 1953 can be found on the Internet. 'Have you been offered a movie contract?' one reporter asked her. 'Yes,' she replied, 'but I haven't accepted it.'

Jorgensen started a career as a singer and actress and her openness and self-confidence have done much for the acceptance of transsexuality. When she told a reporter that from time to time the attention was getting a bit much for her, he suggested she start a new life under a different name. 'My dear,' she said, 'I just did.'

Obviously, despite all the names I have mentioned, not all transwomen work as movie stars. There are transwomen who work in health care, in the police force and in the construction industry. Michelle Duff is a former Grand Prix motorcyclist, Deirdre McCloskey is a renowned economist and Sara Buechner is a famous concert pianist. Anna Grodzka is a member of the Polish parliament, Aya Kamikawa was elected to the city council in Tokyo, and engineer and pilot Amanda Simpson holds an important position in the U.S. Defense Department.

I am personally facinated by the life of Charlotte-Geneviève-Louise-Auguste-Andrée-Timothée d'Éon de Beaumont (1728–1810). Known originally as Charles-Geneviève-Louis-Auguste-André-Timothée d'Éon de Beaumont, Charlotte was a French diplomat and spy who changed her sex role when she was 49 years old. She claimed that she was a woman who had been raised as a boy to ensure her father an heir. After her death it became clear that the Chevalier d'Éon had been born a man.

End

ALL THINGS COME to an end. A transition, too. There comes a moment when you are transmuted, transformed, have crossed to the other side. You are done. All being well, you will continue to change, but then it's purely a matter of physical and mental ageing.

As I was writing this, a book arrived in which American novelist T Cooper wrote about his transition. In *Real Man Adventures*, Cooper describes how hard it is to get the outside world to see you as more than just a transsexual. When one of his novels got on to the *Los Angeles Times* bestseller list, LA *Weekly* magazine sent someone to do a short interview. While they were talking, the interviewer brought up his transition. Cooper explained that, though it wasn't a secret, it wasn't the subject of his novel and that other things were more important. The interviewer nodded understandingly. When the article appeared, she had managed to refer to his gender identity nine times in only 650 words.

That's not going to happen to me, I've decided. Two years from now, people will no longer call me to talk about my body. In one year Wikipedia will start behaving itself and write something informative about my work, rather than ferreting around in my private life. After a lifetime of doubt, I have now passed the Devil's crossroad – shall I? shan't I? – and now I can finally just start living like other people do. I'm looking forward to it.

Acknowledgements and Sources

THE INFORMATION IN this book was partly obtained from the Internet, from the accounts of people whom I won't mention by name, because I don't know if they would appreciate it.

Arguments and examples are taken from my correspondence and from discussions within the international web community of FTMs, people who take the step from Female to Male, and MTFs, those who cross over from Male to Female. Of course, they all have their own experiences, expectations, perspectives and terminology; I make no pretension here of providing an all-encompassing account or summary of these. I would refer anyone who is interested to the many lively discussions on the Internet.

For the chapter on Famous Figures, I made much use of the archives of outhistory.org, blogs.villagevoice.com and library.transgenderzone.com. I have checked the facts in the chapter as best as I could, but many accounts were contradictory, as in the past people did not always dare to tell the truth about their lives. My findings should not therefore be seen as the last word.

Other informative sources

Hudson's FTM Resource Guide
www.ftmguide.org

Lynn Conway's website
http://ai.eecs.umich.edu/people/conway/conway.html
Her article 'Transsexualism is More Common than
you Think', written with Femke Olyslager, can also be
found here

Joanne Herman, *Transgender Explained, for Those Who
Are Not* (Bloomington, IN, 2009)
Herman's book provides practical information based on
the author's own experiences

Stephen Whittle, Lewis Turner, Ryan Combs and
Stephenne Rhodes, *Transgender Eurostudy: Legal Survey
and Focus on the Transgender Experience of Health Care*,
Transgender Europe and ILGA-Europe (2008)
www.pfc.org.uk/pdf/eurostudy.pdf